PRAISE FOR
WRITING A KILLER THRILLER

"Finally, someone who understands the thriller! More than ever an author must also be his own best editor and Jodie Renner is there to help. *Writing a Killer Thriller* should be on every thriller writer's desk. It breaks down the thriller into its must-have component parts to write a scintillating, edge of the seat novel that will get readers buzzing and sales flowing."

— Robert Dugoni, New York Times bestselling author of *The Jury Master* and *Murder One*

"*Writing a Killer Thriller* by Jodie Renner is an in-depth journey through each component of the thriller. Renner breaks down the process into key elements, each essential to keeping the reader turning those pages. From character development to building suspense, *Writing a Killer Thriller* should be on the desk of every thriller author out there. A staple for the beginner, a refresher for the pro."

— Joe Moore, #1 Amazon and international bestselling co-author of *The Blade* and *The Phoenix Apostles*

"Writing is hard, editing harder, and self-editing almost impossible. *Writing a Killer Thriller* demystifies each of these steps on the road to a published manuscript. Read this book. It will help you now and for many years to come."

— DP Lyle, Macavity Award winning and Edgar, Agatha, Anthony, Benjamin Franklin, Scribe, and USA Best Books nominated author of the Dub Walker thriller series

"A killer of a thriller guide! Jodie Renner lays out, in clear, easy steps and lists, how the best writers craft their works of art – and shows how you can do it, too. A terrific how-to in avoiding the pitfalls and burnishing the gotta-haves of writing a bestselling thriller novel, by an editor who knows her way around action, drama and creating characters so fresh and real you'll swear they were your friends."

— **Shane Gericke, national bestselling and No. 1 Kindle bestselling author of *Torn Apart***

"Jodie Renner is a terrific fiction editor who is constantly updating her craft. She's edited several novels for me, and I highly recommend her services and books. Even if you don't write thrillers, her advice is applicable to writing a compelling story in almost any genre."

— **L.J. Sellers, bestselling author of provocative mysteries and thrillers**

"With years of experience as a professional editor to many successful authors, Renner knows what it takes to write a good thriller, and she lays it all out here in a no-nonsense, easy-to-understand manner. From building excitement and suspense on every page, to adding tension and conflict to each chapter, this book is packed with information you simply can't afford to miss if you want to gain that ever-elusive competitive edge in the world of fiction."

— **Andrew E. Kaufman, #1 bestselling author of *The Lion, the Lamb, the Hunted* and *While the Savage Sleeps***

"Jodie Renner has demystified the process of thriller-writing with *Writing a Killer Thriller*. This book is packed full of information which is not just useful, but critical to the success of any thriller writer, whether just starting out or a veteran of many books. [...] If you want to avail yourself of the knowledge of one of the best freelance thriller editors in the business, you couldn't ask for a better deal than *Writing a Killer Thriller*."

— **Allan Leverone, bestselling thriller and horror writer**

WRITING A KILLER THRILLER

*An Editor's Guide
to Writing Compelling Fiction*

Second Edition

JODIE RENNER

*"When it comes to fiction techniques,
Jodie Renner knows her stuff. She's the real deal."*

— D.P. Lyle, MD, Macavity Award-winning and
Edgar Award-nominated author of many
non-fiction and fiction books

Writing a Killer Thriller
– An Editor's Guide to Writing Compelling Fiction
Second Edition

ISBN-13: 978-1490389943
ISBN-10: 1490389946
BISAC: Reference / Writing Skills

Published by Cobalt Books, www.CobaltBooks.net.
Cover Design: Travis Miles, www.ProBookCovers.com
Interior Design: Craig Lancaster, www.Craig-Lancaster.com
Also available in e-book publication
Printed in the United States of America, by CreateSpace

ACKNOWLEDGMENTS

I'd like to thank D.P. Lyle, MD, for inviting me back repeatedly as a guest on his popular blog, *The Writer's Forensics Blog*, where he posted most of the original articles for the first, shorter edition of this book, in 2011–2012.

Of all the writing "gurus" whose books have taught me so much and whom I quote in my books, James Scott Bell and Jessica Page Morrell top the list.

James Scott Bell's books have been my beacon since I started seriously studying the craft of writing compelling fiction about seven years ago. I highly recommend these books by Bell, which I consider indispensable for fiction writers who are serious about perfecting their craft: *Revision & Self-Editing*, *Plot & Structure*, and *Conflict & Suspense*.

I'd also like to thank Jessica Page Morrell, whose writing I've long admired, for giving me the personal advice I needed to start taking my own writing more seriously. I highly recommend Jessica's craft books, *Thanks, But This Isn't for Us* and *Between the Lines*.

Other writing instructors I've learned a great deal from include Randy Ingermanson and Peter Economy, Jack M. Bickham, Donald Maass, James N. Frey, Elizabeth Lyon, Sol Stein, and Hallie Ephron.

Finally, I'd like to thank my many author clients, especially the thriller writers – working with you to make your novels the best they can be forced me to analyze what works and what doesn't, and search for the essential ingredients of a riveting, page-turning novel.

TABLE OF CONTENTS

Introduction

Part VII – REVISE FOR SUCCESS

Part VIII – WRAP-UP & CHECKLISTS

PART IX – OTHER RELATED INFO

INTRODUCTION

Whether you're planning your first novel or revising your fourth, you'll discover lots of concrete ideas here for taking your fiction up a level or two, captivating readers, and gaining fans. Both published and aspiring authors of fast-paced, popular fiction will find these tips indispensable for plotting a riveting story and creating compelling characters, then writing a gripping opening and designing suspenseful scenes. And the reader-friendly format makes it easy to also find tips on picking up the pace, ramping up the tension and intrigue, revising for power, and creating a page-turner that sells.

As a freelance editor who specializes in thrillers and other suspenseful, fast-paced fiction, when I'm not editing, I'm reading bestselling novels, especially suspense-thrillers, or poring over my numerous craft-of-fiction books by industry "gurus" like Donald Maass, James Scott Bell, Jessica Page Morrell, Stephen King, James N. Frey, Jack M. Bickham, and many others. The topics in this book arose from my critical reading of fast-paced fiction, analyzing ideas expressed by leaders in the field, and my editing of thrillers and other fiction.

A companion guide to this one, my *Fire up Your Fiction – An Editor's Guide to Writing Compelling Stories*, is available in both e-book and trade paperback.

If you find this book helpful, I hope you'll take a few minutes to write a review under it on Amazon. Thanks, and keep on writing! I look forward to reading your thriller!

— Jodie Renner,
June 2013

PART I

WHAT'S A THRILLER, ANYWAY?

Chapter 1 – THRILLERS VERSUS MYSTERIES

Until fairly recently, most readers were more familiar with mysteries than thrillers. Mysteries of all sorts (cozy, hardboiled, suspenseful, etc.) are still going strong, but thrillers make up more and more of the bestsellers these days. How exactly do thrillers differ from mysteries, anyway? Both are fiction stories involving criminal activity, catching the bad guy(s), and at least one murder.

Two main differences stand out. First, in a mystery, neither the reader nor the protagonist knows who the killer is. The whole idea is to figure out "whodunit," then apprehend the bad guy. In a thriller, the reader often knows who the villain is early on, and sometimes the hero does too. The object is for the hero to outwit and stop the killer before he kills others, including the hero, or endangers the world. Also, in mysteries, the protagonist is not usually in danger, whereas in thrillers, the protagonist is almost always directly threatened, fighting for his life as he matches wits with a clever, determined, amoral villain.

The other main difference between mysteries and thrillers is in the delivery—how they are told. Mysteries are usually more cerebral, for readers who enjoy solving puzzles, whereas thrillers are more heart-pounding, adrenaline-raising, appealing to the emotions and a yearning for excitement, a desire to vicariously confront danger and defeat nasty villains. A mystery, especially a "cozy" one, can unfold in a leisurely fashion, but thrillers need to be much more fast-paced and suspenseful.

David Morrell, author of 28 thrillers, explored the difference between mysteries and thrillers several years ago. His detailed description included this: "Traditional mysteries appeal primarily to the mind and emphasize the logical solution to a puzzle. In contrast, thrillers strive for heightened emotions and emphasize the sensations of what might be called an obstacle race and a scavenger hunt." (*David Morrell, www.crimespreemag.com*)

James N. Frey, author of *How to Write a Damn Good Thriller* and *How to Write a Damn Good Mystery*, among other "damn good" books on writing, says, "In the United States, mysteries are not considered to be thrillers, though they share some common elements." Frey describes the differences like this: "In a mystery, the hero has a mission to find a killer. In a thriller, the hero has a mission to foil evil."

Frey goes on to elaborate, "a thriller is a story of a hero who has a mission to foil evil. Not just a hero—a clever hero. Not just a mission—an 'impossible' mission. An 'impossible' mission that will put our hero into terrible trouble."

According to International Thriller Writers, a thriller is characterized by "the sudden rush of emotions, the excitement, sense of suspense, apprehension, and exhilaration that drive the narrative, sometimes subtly with peaks and lulls, sometimes at a constant, breakneck pace."

ITW defines thrillers as a genre in which "tough, resourceful, but essentially ordinary heroes are pitted against villains determined to destroy them, their country, or the stability of the free world."

Part of the allure of thrillers, they say, comes from not only what their stories are about but also how they are told. "High stakes, non-stop action, plot twists that both surprise and excite, settings that are both vibrant and exotic, and an intense pace that never lets up until the adrenaline-packed climax."

Here are some distinctions James Scott Bell makes between the two genres in his book *Conflict & Suspense*:

Mystery = Who did it?
Suspense = Will it happen again?
Mystery is about "figuring it out."
Suspense is about "keeping safe."
Mystery is a puzzle.
Suspense is a nightmare.
Mysteries ask, "What will the lead character find next?"
Suspense asks, "What will happen next to the lead character?"

I asked some friends, clients, and colleagues what they thought the main differences were between these two genres. According to my client, thriller and horror writer Allan Leverone, "The definition I like best is this: In a mystery, the crime has already been committed, but the hero and the reader must figure out by whom. In a thriller, the crime (at least the biggie) hasn't been committed yet, but the reader knows who the bad guy is; the question is whether he can be stopped."

Mystery and romance writer Terry Odell says, "The best definition I've heard is that in a mystery, you're one step behind the detective, since you don't know anything until he does. In suspense, you're one step ahead, because you know things that the detective [or hero] can't know." This is especially true when we get into the viewpoint of the villain.

My friend, popular suspense-mystery and thriller writer, LJ Sellers, tells me she recently read that in a thriller, the villain drives the story. That contrasts with a mystery, in which the protagonist drives the story.

And finally, another good friend and colleague, bestselling thriller and horror writer Andrew E. Kaufman says, "Here's a less conservative, completely off-color definition, coming from a less conservative, completely off-color mind: A thriller is like mystery on Viagra. Everything's more amped up, fast-paced, and frenetic. A good thriller should keep your heart racing, your fingers swiping at the pages, and your rear on the edge of its seat. Of course, those lines can be blurred. Many authors straddle the fence between the two. Nothing is in black and white, and gray is a beautiful color."

It's true that some thrillers have a lot of elements of mysteries in them, and vice-versa. Some fast-paced suspense-mysteries that seem to straddle both genres include Robert Crais's Joe Pike and Elvis Cole stories and Harlan Coben's Myron Bolitar series.

I used to read a lot of mysteries, and still do from time to time, but in the last few years I much prefer the excitement and pulse-pounding suspense of thrillers. My favorite thriller writers these days include bestselling authors Robert Crais, Sandra Brown, Lee Child, Karin Slaughter, Michael Connelly, Nora Roberts, Harlan Coben, Lisa Gardner, Dean Koontz, Lisa Scottoline, John Grisham, Allison Brennan, Janet Evanovich, and many more.

For popular thriller or mystery-suspense series, I love following the exploits of engaging, charismatic characters like Joe Pike, D.D. Warren, Jack Reacher, Maggie O'Dell, Elvis Cole, Lucy Kincaid, Harry Bosch, Eve Dallas, Myron Bolitar, Eve Duncan, Jane Rizzoli, and Stephanie Plum — and the two hunks in her life!

PART II

DESIGN A KILLER PLOT

Chapter 2 – KNOW THE BASIC INGREDIENTS OF A KILLER THRILLER

To compete in today's competitive publishing marketplace, your thriller needs clever plotting, with lots of conflict, tension, and suspense, and a few twists and surprises, especially at the end. You need some gripping, heart-pounding scenes, each connected to the next and the story as a whole, with lots of direct cause and effect. And for maximum intrigue and reader satisfaction, it's important to drop little tantalizing details and hints along the way, which all make sense at the end.

For these reasons, it's best to try to sketch out some kind of overall plan or plot list in advance; otherwise, you could get bogged down and drive yourself crazy climbing out of plot holes and rewriting scenes where your story goes off on tangents or just meanders or sputters to a halt.

Your thriller plot needs a solid foundation you can build on, or the whole story could collapse around you in a muddled-up heap. Unless you have at least a major story question/problem in mind, if you just start writing to see where it takes you, you may end up with a lot of "and then...and then...and then..." scenes, with no real point or connection. Not to mention clues that end up going nowhere. This would leave your readers confused and irritated and could sink your reputation as a thriller writer. Even a rough road map will help you stay focused as you're writing. For an excellent overall guide, see the eight-point plot arc in Chapter 3.

WHAT ARE THE INGREDIENTS
OF A RIVETING THRILLER?

James N. Frey sums it up: "To create a damn good thriller, you need to create a clever hero and send him or her on an 'impossible' mission to foil evil for the benefit of others."

Here's another definition of thrillers, from good old Wikipedia: "A broad genre of literature, film, and television programming that uses suspense, tension and excitement as the main elements. Thrillers heavily stimulate the reader's or viewer's moods, giving them a high level of anticipation, ultra-heightened expectation, uncertainty, surprise, anxiety, and/or terror. Thriller films tend to be adrenaline-rushing, gritty, rousing, and fast-paced.

"A thriller provides the sudden rush of emotions, excitement, and exhilaration that drive the narrative, sometimes subtly with peaks and lulls, sometimes at a constant, breakneck pace with thrills. It keeps the audience cliff-hanging at the 'edge of their seats' as the plot builds towards a climax. Literary devices such as red herrings, plot twists, and cliffhangers are used extensively. A thriller is usually a villain-driven plot, whereby he or she presents obstacles that the protagonist must overcome."

You need to get the readers emotionally involved from the very first sentence. Here's how to do it, according to Jessica Page Morrell: "Involvement begins when you create a realistic world, implant an issue that demands to be resolved, and introduce a character or group of characters who are intensely interesting to readers."

Your plot needs:
+ A clever, resourceful, likeable but complex protagonist
+ A conniving, frightening, determined villain
+ An overriding, preferably high-concept problem
+ Other related conflicts
+ Plenty of intrigue, suspense, and tension
+ Some surprises or reversals
+ A final big, very close battle

⋆ A satisfying resolution, with a final twist or surprise, and all the major story questions answered.

Also, your protagonist should have a character arc. He or she is usually not the same person at the end as at the beginning. The challenges and trials of the story have deeply affected them and changed them forever. Series characters tend to have a much less noticeable arc.

WHAT'S HIGH-CONCEPT FICTION?

Here's a list of elements of high-concept stories, which apply to any popular genre, by Jeff Lyons, of Storygeeks.com. This list appeared in the July/August 2013 issue of Writer's Digest magazine:

7 Qualities of High-Concept Stories

1. High level of entertainment value
2. High degree of originality
3. Born from a "what if" question
4. Highly visual
5. Clear emotional focus
6. Inclusion of some truly unique element
7. Mass audience appeal (to a broad general audience or a large niche market)

Lyons adds that most stories don't possess all seven qualities, but the more of them you can identify in your story, the higher the concept.

Lyons lists three thriller/suspense titles that each possess several of the above qualities: *Gone Girl*, by Gillian Flynn; *Suspect*, by Robert Crais; and *Catch Me*, by Lisa Gardner.

For more details and the explanations for each point, check out the magazine article or Jeff Lyons' website, Storygeeks.com.

HOW AND WHERE TO START?

Here are James N. Frey's basic steps for getting started (condensed, and my numbers and bolding):

1. First, find a damn good **germinal idea** that excites you, that sets your blood on fire.

2. Next, create a damn good three-dimensional thriller **villain**.

3. Once you know the villain down to the bone, find his or her **dark mission**. This is the plot behind the plot.

4. Then create a damn good three-dimensional **hero**.

5. Now start planning your story, developing characters and conflicts as you go along.

HOW TO GET IDEAS? WHAT IF?

Watch/read the news every day. Read intriguing novels. Watch exciting movies and TV shows. Play the "What if?" game. Use your imagination to create "What if?" scenarios: What if (your character) picked up the wrong suitcase at the airport and....? What if the cab driver suddenly turned in the wrong direction and told (your character) he had his own plans for her? What if a patient was wheeled into the wrong operating room? What if their daughter went missing from camp? What if accompanying someone on a test drive of your car turned into a nightmare?

Here are a few what if questions for some classic novels or movies. Match them with the titles below.

 • What if dinosaurs were cloned?
 • What if Martians invaded the earth?
 • What if women stopped giving birth?
 • What if a gigantic rogue shark terrorized a small island community?

The Children of Men, Jurassic Park, Jaws, The War of the Worlds

Brainstorm every day, on your daily commute or walk, in the shower, and when you're dropping off to sleep and waking up. Write your "What if?" ideas down as you think of them, or use your smartphone or other little recorder to record them while you're driving, etc.

Pick a few of your favorite "What if?" questions, then build on them to see where you can take them. To turn your initial "What if?" question into a bestselling thriller, you'll need to keep probing and adding depth by asking more questions, applying pressure to your character, and adding on more dilemmas and conflict. In there you'll come up with a villain. Keep escalating the initial idea by continually raising the stakes until you have five or six sentences or a half page that can form the basis for a whole novel.

WHAT'S THE PREMISE OF YOUR STORY?

What's your story basically about? What's your main story problem or question? Can you state it in three or four sentences? Fill this in before you start writing, so you have a clear picture in your mind of your hero's main challenge to guide you as you go along:

(Protagonist's name) is a _____ who _____. But (first big encounter/conflict/problem). Now (action sentence). Will (big dilemma, question)?

It's important to have a short, sweet "elevator pitch," an intriguing description of your story that you will use when people ask you, "So what's your story about, anyway?" Or in case you're at a writers' conference and you end up in the elevator with your dream agent. You have only a few floors to convince them that your story is fascinating – make every word count! (But don't try this in the restrooms, unless you want to get on their blacklist!)

Now try to tell what your story is about in one sentence – your storyline.
If you didn't do the "What if?" exercise above, try now to express your storyline as a "What if?" question, with a maximum of two or three sentences.

This would be a good time to run your basic premise and story outline past some smart friends or a critique group, just to be sure there aren't any major flaws in your basic concept that would create huge, embarrassing plot holes down the road. It's much better to work through the logistics now rather than after you've put hundreds of hours into writing the story!

CHARACTER-DRIVEN OR PLOT-DRIVEN?

Should your thriller mainly be focused on the main character's quest, challenges, and problems? Or should the character be secondary to the plot? Psychological thrillers are of course character-driven, as are many other subgenres to greater or lesser degrees. And it's often the villain who drives the plot more than the hero or heroine, who are reacting to the threats.

Unless you're writing a military or techno thriller or a tough action-adventure, which are generally plot-driven, it's usually best to go for a character-driven plot, where readers identify closely with the hero or heroine and follow their journey with trepidation, rooting for them every step of the way. Focusing on your character's journey and struggles, showing us how they're managing to cope at every turn, creates greater reader involvement.

A little tip for writers who don't like to plot the whole story in advance:

One approach I've seen advocated several times is to plan your beginning and ending and main story question/conflict and a few plot points in between, then start by writing your ending (even if it changes later), then write your opening, then your second-to-last scene, then your second scene, then continue as you like.

Resources:
James N. Frey, *How to Write a Damn Good Thriller*
Jeff Lyons, Storygeeks.com, article in Writer's Digest magazine
Jessica Page Morrell, *Between the Lines*

Chapter 3 – BUILD YOUR STORY ON A SOLID FOUNDATION

WHY WORRY ABOUT STRUCTURE AT ALL?

Your story needs some kind of general blueprint so it doesn't meander all over the place, darting here and there, trying this and that, confusing the readers, then sputtering and dying. Or overwhelming the readers with violence, chases and explosives, with no real point or substance. Without some kind of general storytelling guidelines as underpinnings to focus your plot and provide reader satisfaction, the possibilities of getting bogged down and confusing or annoying your readers are endless,

SOME BASIC PLOT AND STRUCTURE GUIDELINES

There are all kinds of excellent craft-of-writing books out there (see my list of resources at the end of this book) that go into detail on how to plot and structure a compelling novel that sells, including a great book devoted entirely to this subject, *Plot & Structure*, by James Scott Bell, so for this guide, I'll just briefly outline various plot structures and how they relate to writing a thriller or other fast-paced fiction.

MYTHIC STRUCTURE – THE HERO'S JOURNEY

This age-old structure from the earliest tales, first described by Joseph Campbell in 1949, outlines the basic steps of a mythic tale, many of which still apply to modern-day thrillers. Although much more complex and detailed than this, the hero's journey can be simplified into these rough steps:

1. We are introduced to the hero in his normal world.
2. The hero is challenged – a "call to adventure."
3. The hero faces a difficult decision whether to accept the challenge or try to ignore it.
4. The hero "crosses the threshold" into a dark world to confront evil.
5. The hero faces various challenges and gets into various battles with forces of evil.
6. The hero has a "dark moment," where he is challenged to the maximum and must overcome doubts and fears in order to continue.
7. The final battle is fought.
8. The hero is victorious and returns to his own world – "the crossing of the return threshold."

THE CLASSICAL THREE-ACT STRUCTURE

Most writing "gurus" recommend the tried-and-true three-act structure, which has provided a secure framework for adventure stories since the beginning of storytelling. The three acts are basically the beginning, the middle, and the end.

ACT I, OR THE BEGINNING

This section, roughly the first quarter of most novels, but often shorter in thrillers (first fifth or sixth of the book), comprises the hook and setup, where you:

• Introduce your main character (as soon as possible, preferably in the first paragraph) – who.
• Present the protagonist's world – what, where, when.
• Establish the tone and style for this book.
• Disrupt your hero's world. Show, almost immediately, the first event or action that causes a disturbance in the protagonist's world.
• Complicate things more. Add a bigger problem, the first big threat that poses the main story question and compels the protagonist to take on the major challenge.

• Introduce the main opponent of the story.

This first act needs lots of tension, conflict, and intrigue, to drive the story forward and keep readers turning the pages.

Act I ends with the threatened protagonist forced into making a difficult choice and going through what James Scott Bell calls "the first door of no return," into the second act.

ACT II, THE MIDDLE

Your protagonist is now committed to the battle. This section, which makes up about half of your story, is the heart of it, where the main confrontations and most of the complications take place. This is the "cauldron" or "crucible" the hero is stuck in – he can't go back and can only move forward.

Act II is where you continually heighten the conflict and tension, throwing your hero increasing challenges and troubles, forcing him to draw more and more on courage and resourcefulness he didn't even know he had.

Also, deepen relationships with your protagonist and other people in her world and develop any subplots in this section.

Near the end of Act II, create a turn of events that sets up the final confrontation of Act III. It might be a huge setback for the hero, or a major discovery fraught with danger. Or a major piece of information, an epiphany or revelation that compels the protagonist forward to finally defeat evil, protect innocents from danger, and restore justice. Your hero or heroine can't turn back at this point and is forced to go through what Bell calls "the second door of no return."

ACT III, THE ENDING

This section, about the last quarter or fifth of your thriller, is where your hero is challenged to the max, in a life-or-death struggle with the villain. It's your hero's darkest moment.

The cunning villain almost wins, but the hero manages to defeat him at the last minute in a nail-biting climax.

Finally, the main story questions are answered and any loose ends tied up in a quick resolution. Leave the reader with some resonance, a sense of satisfaction, and the desire to read another novel by you.

FREYTAG'S FIVE-ACT DRAMATIC STRUCTURE

In 1863, Gustav Freytag, a German, advanced his theory of a five-act dramatic or narrative structure that divided a story into five parts: exposition, rising action, climax (or turning point), falling action, and resolution. Here's a brief explanation of each of the five main parts of a story, according to Freytag:

1. Exposition – Story Setup
The exposition introduces all of the main characters in the story and shows how they relate to one another, what their goals and motivations are, and the kind of people they are. Most importantly, the audience gets to know the main character, and the protagonist gets to know his or her main goal and what is at stake if he or she fails to attain it.

2. Rising action – Initial Problems, Conflicts
The rising action shows the initial conflict and early issues – the first struggles of the main character. The protagonist now understands his main goal and begins to work toward it, and begins his struggle against the antagonist. Smaller problems thwart any initial success, and in this phase his progress is directed primarily against these secondary obstacles. This phase shows us how he overcomes these obstacles.

3. Climax – Turning Point – Major Confrontation
The point of climax is the turning point of the story, where the main character makes the single big decision that defines the outcome of the story and who he is as a person. This stage occupies the middle of the story.

The beginning of this phase is marked by the protagonist finally having cleared away the preliminary barriers and being ready to engage with the adversary. Usually, entering this phase, both the protagonist and the antagonist have a plan to win against the other. Now for the first time we see them going against one another in direct, or nearly direct, conflict.

This struggle results with neither character completely winning, nor losing, against the other. Usually, each character's plan is partially successful, and partially foiled by his adversary. What is unique about this central struggle between the two characters is that the protagonist makes a decision that shows us his moral quality, and ultimately determines his fate.

The climax often contains much of the action in a story, for example, a defining battle.

4. Falling action – Dark Moment
This is often the time of greatest overall tension, with almost everything going wrong for the protagonist.

In this phase, the villain has the upper hand. It seems that evil will triumph. The protagonist has never been further from accomplishing the goal.

5. Resolution or Denouement
Calling on his last reserves of strength and courage, the hero manages to win the final battle. The main conflict is resolved; the protagonist is (usually) successful; the main story question is answered; all elements of mystery are solved.

NIGEL WATTS' EIGHT-POINT STORY ARC

I recently discovered Nigel Watts' very useful "Eight-Point Story Arc," a time-honored, foolproof way to structure a story, whether it's flash fiction, a short story, a novella, or a novel.

As Watts explains, every classic plot passes through these stages, in this order. You would go through these stages once only for a short story. For a novel, the overall plot should follow this process, and it should also be used on a smaller scale for each subplot within the main story.

You can use this plot structure both at the initial planning stage and as a reference and reminder during the writing process, as Watts does:

"I find it most useful as a checklist against which to measure a work in progress. If I sense a story is going wrong, I see if I've unwittingly missed out a stage of the eight-point arc. It may not guarantee you write a brilliant story, but it will help you avoid some of the pitfalls of a brilliant idea gone wrong."

So what do the eight points mean?

1. Stasis
This is the protagonist in his everyday life, before he's thrown into turmoil.

2. Trigger
A conflict or problem beyond the control of the protagonist (hero/heroine) disturbs his or her world and forces action, setting the story in motion.

Watts' Story Arc

1. Stasis
2. Trigger
3. The quest
4. Surprise
5. Critical choice
6. Climax
7. Reversal
8. Resolution

3. The quest
The trigger, usually a stressful one, forces the protagonist to get involved, make decisions, and act. The main character's quest or goal is usually to solve the problem and return to the status quo or a happy, normal life.

4. Surprise
This stage, which should be called "Surprises," takes up most of the middle part of the story. The surprises usually consist of piling on obstacles, complications, conflict, and trouble for the protagonist. It's a good idea to plant one major plot twist around the middle of your story.

And be sure your surprises aren't predictable or random—they need to be unexpected, but plausible. The reader has to think, *I should have seen that coming!*

5. Critical choice

Just before the climax, your protagonist is forced to make a crucial decision, a critical choice. This decision is highly stressful for your character, who must reach deep within himself for inner resources and plumb the depths of his courage and resolve. This is often called the "dark moment," as the character faces what is likely to be the most difficult decision of his life to this point. The critical choice usually involves a moral dilemma, with the morally right decision being the more difficult path, and the bad decision being the easier one.

This is often when we find out exactly who a character is, as darker traits are revealed at moments of high stress. And of course this needs to be a decision the character must make to take a particular path, not just something that happens by chance.

6. Climax

The critical choice made by your protagonist leads to the climax, the highest peak of tension, in your story. In thrillers, this is the major confrontation and battle between the hero/heroine and villain. It could also involve a high-speed chase or other dramatic happening.

7. Reversal

The reversal is the consequence of the critical choice and the climax, and it shows a major change in the status or outlook of the characters – especially your protagonist. Your hero or heroine has made a big decision and gone through a confrontation, both of which have changed them and their life. Or a story event takes a new, unexpected direction.

Note that your story reversal needs to be believable and inevitable, not the result of a freak accident or a coincidence. And for greatest reader satisfaction, your hero needs to be the master of his own fate and resolve the conflict through summoning his own courage, determination and abilities, not by sheer luck or another character coming to the rescue.

8. Resolution

The resolution is a return to a fresh start – the protagonist has undergone significant changes and is wiser, and can now return to her "normal" life (at least for a while), as the main story problem has been solved and the big story question has been answered.

Nigel Watts of course goes into a great deal more detail in his book, *Teach Yourself – Writing a Novel*, and includes lots of excellent examples from well-known fiction to illustrate each stage in his story plot outline. Watts also discusses many more excellent fiction-writing techniques in this great guide.

PLANNING YOUR NOVEL

Make a rough outline of your plot.

To guide you, start with a plot **outline** or **step sheet**.

Brainstorm and list the main plot points of your story, outlining the main scenes depicting your hero's struggles. These main events should be linked by cause and effect. This gives you a rough framework. You don't have to stick with your outline religiously, but it gives you a good starting point and can focus you again if/when you wonder where you were going. If you decide to change the story in various places, just make the changes on your step sheet, too.

See Chapter 5 for more details on step sheets and how to write them. You don't have to stick with your outline religiously, but it gives you a good starting point and can focus you again if/when you wonder where you were going. If you decide to change the story in various places, just make the changes on your step sheet, too.

Resources:
James Scott Bell, *Plot & Structure*
James N. Frey, *How to Write a Damn Good Thriller*
Nigel Watts, *Teach Yourself – Writing a Novel*, 2006 edition
Wikipedia

Chapter 4 – AVOID THESE PLOT AND STRUCTURE GAFFES

PLOT AND STRUCTURE NO-NO'S TO FIND AND FIX

Here are some possible "big-picture" problems in a thriller or other suspense novel that can be caused by lack of planning. These types of glaring mistakes in plot/structure will bog down your story and could sink your reputation as a thriller writer. Fortunately, they can all be remedied in the revision and self-editing stages.

Overwriting. Not enough self-editing (verbal diarrhea)

Today's bestselling thrillers are mostly between 70,000 and 90,000 words. Unless you're an absolutely brilliant writer, and experts in the business have told you so, if your manuscript is over 95,000 words long, it needs tightening up.

Meandering writing – the main story question / problem is fuzzy

What's the protagonist's main goal and fear, and his main problem? This should be obvious early on and be the overriding driving force behind your whole plot. Don't let it get lost in meandering writing, too much backstory, frequent info dumps, too many characters, too many subplots, and unrelated plot details. As Jessica Page Morrell advises, "weigh each scene and event you include and ask yourself if it's pushing the protagonist toward his goal or opposing his goal. If not, get rid of it."

One unrelated thing after another happens
Don't get caught up in "and then, and then, and then," with a bunch of sub-stories or episodes that aren't related to each other and don't directly tie in with the main plot problem and story question. Your events and scenes need to be connected by cause and effect. Each scene should impact the following scenes and complicate future events.

Dog's breakfast
A common problem is too many characters crowding the scenes with no elbow room, and readers getting confused and frustrated trying to remember who's who. Or maybe you have too many sub-plots that veer off in different directions and confuse the issue. Or a convoluted story where many issues or subplots don't tie in with the main character and their main problem. These issues would all qualify as prime "kill your darlings" material.

A main character that's flat, unsympathetic, predictable, or wishy-washy
Readers want a protagonist they can bond with and root for. Create a lead character who is smart, likeable, and charismatic, but with inner conflict and a few flaws.

A thin plot
This is where the story line is obscure, with all kinds of unrelated happenings and way too much yak-yak dialogue that doesn't have enough tension, conflict, or purpose. Also, often the issues and stakes aren't serious enough. Anything that doesn't directly relate to your major story problem or develop your characters or drive the story forward should be cut.

A predictable story line
Write in some twists, surprises, reversals. When a character has to make a decision or her actions cause repercussions, brainstorm for all possible consequences and choose one readers won't be expecting. Add in reversals here and there that force a change in goals, actions, reactions, or consequences. Don't overdo this, though, and be sure your reversal makes sense and is in character, or your readers will feel manipulated or cheated.

Flat scenes

When scenes are boring, it's because there's not enough friction, worry, and uncertainty. Make sure every page has conflict and tension. Every scene needs a focal point or a "hot spot" – its own mini-climax. Also, be sure to start scenes late and end early. And don't tie everything up with a neat little bow at the end. End with the protagonist in more trouble (most of the time), or with a cliffhanger.

Don't worry, be happy

Everybody's getting along so well. What's wrong with that? It's great in real life, but in fiction it's the kiss of death. Why? Because it's boring. Conflict is what drives fiction forward and keeps readers turning the pages.

Overkill: Nonstop action

Unrelenting car chases, explosions, and violence, with a constant break-neck pace, can numb readers and movie-goers alike.

Here's some good writing advice from a movie review of *Iron Man 3* in *The Weekly Standard*: "What all these moments had in common is that they were unexpected. They had levity and grace, all the more so because they interrupted a series of frenetic action sequences that, in their relentlessness, would have turned enervatingly banal without them.

"So what the audiences crave is not action-movie sameness, but character-driven idiosyncrasies."

The fix: Vary your pacing, and write in some quieter moments here and there for variety and breathing space before the next onslaught.

Plot holes

Watch for those actions, reactions, events, character reactions, and other details that just don't make sense for one reason or another. Look for any inconsistencies, illogical details, or discrepancies. Make sure all your story questions are answered at some point.

These internal content/logistic errors are often difficult for the author to see, so this is where your critique group or beta readers can be invaluable, especially if you specifically ask them to flag anything that doesn't make sense for any reason, no matter how big or small.

Better yet, you can save yourself a lot of time and frustration by running your basic plot line past a few smart, trusted friends before you even start writing, in case they say something like, "Well, I don't see how that could even work, because..." Then you can reexamine the overall premise or plot idea for plausibility and fix any glaring logistics errors early on.

A sagging middle
It's easy to get bogged down in the middle and turn it into a muddle.

Your middle needs:

• Escalating conflict, stakes continually rising for the protagonist
• Surprises, difficulties, twists, setbacks, and complications that challenge the protagonist and keep the readers turning pages
• Increasing threats by the bad guy(s)
• A ticking clock – time constraints, to add pressure and tension

A strategy to remedy this: If you're getting bogged down and losing interest/inspiration, go back to where the story really grabbed you, and consider what came between that and the scene you're at now. How can you oomph up the scenes in between? Should the less-than-compelling section be revised or even cut and replaced with a more gripping scene or series of scenes? (Remember to save anything you take out for possible future use.)

No noticeable character arc
With the exception of a lot of action-adventure or military stories, and Lee Child's Jack Reacher novels, most compelling thrillers show the main character undergoing change, caused by the adversity they've gone through and the resources they had to pull out of themselves to survive or conquer evil. Usually they are stronger and more confident for it and more able to face adversity. Certain attitudes they held at the beginning will often have changed by the end, especially negative ones. Even minor character growth and enlightenment will be satisfying to readers, who've become bonded with that person.

An unsatisfying ending

This can be caused by a number of factors, such as:

• The hero wins by a coincidence, act of God, or help from a minor character. We want the hero to win by his own resourcefulness, cleverness, determination, courage, and inner strength! Not by help from others or Deus ex machina.

• The hero loses. Unsatisfying and disappointing. Leave that for literary fiction. Or if you must make him lose the last battle, make him win/gain in another way.

• Ending is too predictable. Brainstorm for possible ways to add a surprise twist at the end.

• Logic flaws – the ending doesn't really make sense given the details supplied earlier.

• Things wrap up too tidily and suddenly. Don't be in a hurry to finish your story – make sure all the story questions are addressed and all the elements of the ending make sense.

• Things dribbling on for too long after the resolution. Know when to stop.

To guard against or remedy these kinds of gaffes, be sure to enlist some knowledgeable beta readers who read bestselling thrillers for pleasure. And whether you're planning to pitch your story to agents and acquiring editors or publish it yourself, it's important to contact a well-respected freelance editor with good credentials and references to go over your manuscript.

Resources:

James N. Frey, *How to Write a Damn Good Thriller*
James Scott Bell, *Plot & Structure*
Jessica Page Morrell, *Thanks, But This Isn't for Us*
Movie review in *The Weekly Standard*: http://www.weeklystandard.com/keyword/Iron-Man-3-Review

PART III

CREATE
COMPELLING
CHARACTERS

Chapter 5 – INVENT A CHARISMATIC HERO

The hero or heroine of a suspense-thriller, like the protagonist of any popular bestseller, has to be impassioned, unique, and likeable enough for the reader to be immediately drawn to them and want to follow them through their journey, worrying about them and cheering them on through their challenges. So it's important to take the time to create a charismatic, passionate, complex, sympathetic main character, so readers connect with him or her immediately.

Heroes in novels and movies haven't really changed a lot since the days of Robin Hood and Maid Marion, but they continue to have universal appeal because, through them, readers can vicariously participate in exciting adventures, confront danger, and defeat evil to win the day and restore justice. Makes for a very entertaining, satisfying read. Get the adrenaline flowing with worry and fear, then triumph over adversity together, just in the nick of time!

Like the heroes of tales of long ago and, more recently, western and action-adventure stories and movies, the hero of a thriller is often larger than life, and because of his cleverness, determination and special skills, can accomplish feats most of us cannot, including finding and crushing the bad guys before they get him! But unless you're writing a James Bond-type story, don't make your hero perfect or too cocky! Give them some inner conflict, baggage, and insecurities to keep readers identifying with them and worrying about them.

What's the basic recipe for a suspense hero or heroine that sells books? The ideal hero is clever, resourceful, charismatic, likeable, tenacious, and courageous – but not perfect. They may be an ordinary person whose life is suddenly thrown into turmoil and they're forced to reach deep inside themselves to find courage and resources they never knew they had. Or the hero may be (and often is) a rebel who defies society's rules, but he has inner integrity and a personal code of honor, and will risk his life for a worthy cause. Readers want to cheer him on to defeat evil, so they can get a sense of satisfaction that they, too, could stop the bad guys, help innocent victims, and restore harmony to their scary world.

From my various reading of craft-of-fiction books and bestselling thrillers, and my own editing of thrillers and other suspense fiction, I've come up with this list of desired qualities for the hero or heroine of a page-turning suspenseful mystery, romantic suspense, or thriller novel.

ATTRIBUTES OF A BESTSELLING HERO OR HEROINE

Clever
They need to be smart enough to figure out the clues and outsmart the villain. Readers don't want to feel they're smarter than the lead character. They don't want to say, "Oh, come on! Figure it out, already!"

Resourceful
Think MacGyver, Katniss of *The Hunger Games*, Harry Potter, Indiana Jones, Jason Bourne, or Dr. Richard Kimble of *The Fugitive*. The hero needs to be able to use ingenuity and whatever's at his disposal to get out of any jams he finds himself in and also to find and defeat the bad guy(s).

Experienced
They've done things and been places. They've had a variety of tough life experiences that have helped them grow. They've "lived" and are stronger and more resilient for it. They're definitely not timid or naïve.

Determined
Your hero or heroine needs to be tenacious and resilient. They keep going. They don't cave under pressure or adversity. They have a goal and stick to it, despite personal discomforts like fatigue, hunger, injuries, and threats.

Courageous

Bravery is essential, as readers want to look up to him/her. Any heroes who are tentative or fearful early on should soon find courage they didn't know they had. The challenges and dangers they face force them to be stronger, creating growth and an interesting character arc.

Physically fit

Your heroine or hero should be up to the physical challenges facing her/him. It's more believable if they jog or work out regularly, like Joe Pike running uphill carrying a 40-pound backpack. (Okay, maybe that's an extreme example.) Don't lose reader credibility by making your character perform feats you haven't already built into their makeup, abilities you can't justify by what we know about them so far.

Skilled

To defeat those clever, skilled villains, they almost always have some special skills and talents to draw on when the going gets rough. For example, Katniss in Hunger Games is a master archer and knows how to track and survive in the woods, Jack Reacher has his army police training, size, and intellect to draw on, and Joe Pike has multiple talents, including patience and stealth.

Charismatic

Attractive in some way. Fascinating, appealing, and enigmatic. Maybe even sexy. People are drawn to him or her, and readers will be, too.

Confident but not overly cocky

Stay away from arrogant, unless you're going for unrealistic caricatures like James Bond.

Passionate, but not overly emotional

Often calm under fire, steadfast. Usually don't break under pressure. Often intense about what they feel is right and wrong, but "the strong, silent type" is common among current popular thrillers – "a man of few words," like Joe Pike or Jack Reacher or Harry Bosch.

Unique, unpredictable
They usually have a special worldview and a distinctive background and attitude that set them apart from others. They'll often act in surprising ways, which keeps their adversaries off-balance and the readers on edge.

Complex
Imperfect, with some inner conflict. Guard against having a perfect or invincible hero or heroine. Make them human, with some self-doubt and fear, so readers worry more about the nasty villains defeating them and get more emotionally invested in their story.

Wounded
Had a tough background that toughened them up somewhat. But they're still vulnerable because of it. Lucy Kincaid, from Allison Brennan's romantic thriller series, was brutally attacked and nearly killed by a rapist, but she's determined to overcome the emotional scars and become an FBI agent. Joe Pike was repeatedly beaten by an abusive father; Elvis Cole was abandoned by his mother; Jack Reacher was an army brat who was constantly in fights and lost his parents and brother. How these characters deal with their emotional and physical wounds touches the reader's heart and draws us in.

Idealistic, Honorable, Self-sacrificing
The thriller hero or heroine may on occasion lie, cheat, steal, even kill, but they do it for the greater good, to stop threats and defeat evil. While never a pious goody-goody, the thriller hero is prepared to do whatever it takes to help innocent people who are threatened, protect an individual or family being terrorized, or rescue a child who's been kidnapped. Having a sense of honor or being self-sacrificing is often what separates a flawed hero from a villain. For example, Rick in Casablanca is a cad-type antihero who ultimately sacrifices his own personal needs and desires for the greater good and turns into a hero at the end. Similarly with Walt Kowalski, the gruff, racist Clint Eastwood character in *Gran Torino*.

Often a loner or a rebel
Might even be an outlaw. Your hero works well – even best – alone, especially if an undercover agent or on a mission or assignment.

Heroes often find themselves in situations where they can't really depend on others – they need to solve the problems through their own resourcefulness, physical effort, and courage. As a result, and because of their inner makeup, heroes often make their own rules. Some examples of this are Robin Hood, Jesse James, Butch Cassidy and the Sundance Kid, Jack Reacher, and Joe Pike.

Usually likeable
But not always. Exceptions are those really rough, gruff antiheroes who redeem themselves somehow at the end, like Rick in *Casablanca*, Harry Callahan in *Dirty Harry*, or Walt in *Gran Torino*.

Also, it's a good idea to give your hero or heroine:

An Achilles' heel
A weakness or phobia. Maybe they're afraid of heights or are claustrophobic. Maybe they're afraid of snakes, like Indiana Jones. And Superman had to stay away from kryptonite. Give your hero a phobia or weakness, then of course put them in a scene where they'll have to face their fears and overcome them!

A soft spot
Show a softer, more caring side to your tough hero now and then, to make him more human and appealing. Maybe he cares about the underdog, a minor character, an animal, or a child or baby.

Now it's up to you to build a background for your hero that will turn him or her into the kind of person who possesses most of these attributes. Good luck!

Resources:
James Scott Bell, *Revision & Self-Editing*
James N Frey, *How to Write a Damn Good Thriller*
Jodie's reading and editing of bestselling thrillers

Chapter 6 – DEVISE A WORTHY ANTAGONIST

You've outlined a plot and created an appealing, complex protagonist for your thriller or other crime/action fiction – great start! But what about your antagonist? According to James N. Frey, "the villain is your best friend, because the villain creates the plot behind the plot – the plot that has to be foiled by the hero."

CREATE A CUNNING, DETERMINED VILLAIN

The hero or heroine of your suspense novel needs a worthy opponent who is at least as tough and clever as the protagonist – often more so. As James Scott Bell says, "Without a strong opponent, most novels lack that crucial emotional experience for the reader: worry. If it seems the hero can take care of his problems easily, why bother to read on?" The villain usually poses the initial threat that sets off the whole plot, so make sure he's complex, capable, well-motivated, and determined.

And thrillers and other crime fiction need a downright nasty bad guy – but not a "mwoo-ha-ha" caricature or stereotype. If your villain is just a wicked cardboard caricature of what he could be, he'll come off as an old-fashioned cliché, and your readers will quickly lose interest.

To create a believable, complex, chilling villain, make him evil, clever and determined, but also someone who feels justified in his actions. Ask yourself what the bad guy wants and why, how he thinks the protagonist is standing in his way, and how he explains his own motivations to himself.

How does your villain rationalize his actions? He may feel that he is justified because of early childhood abuse or neglect, a grudge against society, a goal thwarted by the protagonist, a desire for revenge against a perceived wrong, or a need for power or status – or money to fund his escape. Whatever his reasons, have them clear in your own mind, and at least hint at them in your novel. Like the protagonist, the antagonist needs clear motivations for his actions.

To give yourself the tools to create a realistic, believable antagonist, create a mini-biography of your villain: his upbringing and family life, early influences, and harrowing experiences or criminal activities so far. Even more effective is to write it in first-person form, as diary entries filled with complaints, resentments, rants and plans to get even. As Hallie Ephron advises us, "Think about what happened to make that villain the way he is. Was he born bad, or did he sour as a result of some traumatic event? If your villain has a grudge against society, why? If he can't tolerate being jilted, why?" No need to share your villain's whole life story with your reader – in fact, I advise against it. But to create a complex, interesting villain, you need to know what drives him to think and act the way he does. Creating a backstory for your antagonist will help you develop a multidimensional, convincing bad guy.

Many writing gurus advise us to even make the antagonist a bit sympathetic. James Scott Bell says, "The great temptation in creating bad guys is to make them evil through and through. You might think this will make your audience root harder for your hero. More likely, you're just going to give your book a melodramatic feel. To avoid this, get to know all sides of your bad guy, including the positives."

Bell suggests that, after we create a physical impression of our antagonist, we find out what her objective is, dig into her motivation, and create background for her that generates some sympathy – a major turning point from childhood or a powerful secret that can emerge later in the book.

Not everyone agrees with that approach, however. James Frey says, "in some cases, it is neither necessary nor perhaps even desirable to create the villain as a fully fleshed-out, well-rounded multidimensional character." Many readers just want to a bad guy they can despise and are not interested in finding out about his inner motives or his deprived childhood. That would dilute their satisfaction in finally seeing him getting his just deserts.

However, Frey does feel it's extremely important to create a convincing, truly nasty villain, one who is "ruthless, relentless, and clever and resourceful, as well as being a moral and ethical wack job," and one who is "willing to crush anyone who gets in his way."

As kids, we loved to see good prevail over evil, and the nastier the villain, the harder they fell – and the greater our satisfaction. Perhaps Frey's "damn good villain" harks back to those times, and his ultimate demise evokes greater reader satisfaction. Forget analyzing the bad guy – just build him up, then take him out!

On the other hand, many readers today are more sophisticated and want to get away from the caricatures of our popular literary heritage; hence, advice from writers like Ephron and Bell to develop more multidimensional antagonists with a backstory and clear motivations.

I'd say there's room for both approaches in modern fiction, and probably the thriller genre favors the "just plain mean and nasty" villain. Unless you're writing a psychological thriller, maybe don't get too carried away with a psychological analysis of the bad guy, although you do need to flesh him out and make him multi-dimensional and believable. But most readers don't want to feel sympathetic toward the villain – they just want to see Jack Reacher, Joe Pike or [fill in your favorite thriller hero or heroine] take them on and kick their butt!

Resources:
Hallie Ephron, *The Everything Guide to Writing Your First Novel*
James N. Frey, *How to Write a Damn Good Thriller*
James Scott Bell, *Revision and Self-Editing*

PART IV

HOOK 'EM
AND KEEP 'EM
WITH TENSION
AND INTRIGUE

Chapter 7 – CRAFT A KILLER OPENING

You've created a compelling protagonist, sympathetic but with inner conflict and baggage, and a creepy, cunning adversary. You've brainstormed "what-ifs" and have come up with a big story quandary with an interesting plot. You've thrust your hero or heroine into one nail-biting scene after another. Now it's time to go back and revise your opening pages to make them as riveting and intriguing as they can be.

I can't emphasize enough how critical your first pages are. They can literally make or break your sales for that book – and maybe future ones. Why? Because after glancing at the front and back cover, potential readers, agents, publishers, and buyers will read your opening page or two to decide whether or not to buy your book. Readers today are busier and less patient, and with all the excellent books out there, if they're not intrigued by the first few pages, they'll reject yours and go on to another.

As James N. Frey says, "A gripping opening is not simply a good thing for your story. It's absolutely essential."

But of course don't get hung up on crafting a brilliant opening right away. First, just get your ideas down and write your story, or most of it, then come back to your opening later, to fine-tune it, amp it up, and polish it to perfection.

SO WHAT ARE THE ESSENTIAL INGREDIENTS OF A GRIPPING OPENING?

Your first page – in fact, your first paragraph – needs to immerse your readers in the story right away, engage them emotionally, and hook them in so they not only want to but need to continue.

> Death is my beat. I make my living from it. I forge my
> professional reputation on it. I treat it with the passion
> and precision of an undertaker...
> – Michael Connelly, opening lines for *The Poet*

For that to happen, several factors come into play.

Tell us whose story it is. First, readers want to know right away
who's the protagonist, the one we'll be rooting for. Put is in the head
of the main character in the first sentence, certainly the first paragraphs. Readers expect that the first person they meet is the one
they'll identify with and bond with, so start right out in the point of
view of your lead character.

> Chris Mankowski's last day on the job, two in the after-
> noon, two hours to go, he got a call to dispose of a bomb.
> – Elmore Leonard, first sentence of *Freaky Deaky*

Situate us right away. And readers want to know immediately
where and when that first scene is taking place, and what's going
on. So be sure you've answered the four W's within the first few
paragraphs: who, what, where, and when – and in an engaging way.
Don't confuse or annoy your readers right off the bat by making
them wonder who's the main person in the story, what's going on at
that moment, and where and when it's happening.

> Penny Dawson woke and heard something moving fur-
> tively in the dark bedroom.
> – Dean Koontz, *Darkfall*

But not in a happy scene. Introduce some tension and conflict
right away. Your lead character wants or needs something and it's
not happening. She's starting to get stressed because...

> Tuesday was a fine California day, full of sunshine and
> promise, until Harry Lyon had to shoot someone at lunch.
> – Dean Koontz, *Dragon Tears*

Make us care about your protagonist. Give readers a hero they'll really want to root for and worry about. He should be sympathetic, interesting, and charismatic, but with inner conflict and baggage. Show us his hopes, dreams, worries, and fears as soon as you can.

> I'd never given much thought to how I would die – even though I'd had reason enough in the last few months – but even if I had, I would not have imagined it like this.
> – Stephenie Meyer, first line of *Twilight*

Give us characters in action. Don't start with your heroine alone, contemplating her life – at least not for long. That's too static and just not engaging or dynamic enough. It's best to put her right away or very soon into a compelling scene with someone else, in real time, with tension, dialogue, actions, and reactions. That way, we get a feel for her personality and a glimpse into her world and her place in it.

> "Well, look what the cat dragged in," Marla Simms bellowed, giving Sara a pointed look over her silver-rimmed bifocals. The secretary for the police station held a magazine in her arthritic hands, but she set it aside, indicating she had plenty of time to talk.
>
> Sara forced some cheer into her voice, though she had purposefully timed her visit for Marla's coffee break. "Hey, Marla. How're you doing?"
> – Karin Slaughter, first two paragraphs of *Indelible*

Avoid neutral, detached descriptions or explanations. Don't address the readers as an omniscient narrator, telling us about the setting, the weather, or the hero from afar. In fact, don't tell us anything on the first pages – show us what's going on through the actions and dialogue of your characters. Filter the descriptions of your hero's surroundings through his perceptions, reactions, mood, and attitude.

> Ford saw the vultures from a half mile off; noticed them wheeling over the island like leaves in a summer thermal,

dozens of black shapes spiraling, and he thought, What in the hell has Bafe got himself into this time?
– Randy Wayne White, beginning of *Sanibel Flats*

Set the tone for the whole book. Your opening paragraphs need to establish the overall tone and mood of this story. Readers need to get a feel early on as to what they're getting into, not only in terms of character and plot but also from your overall approach and attitude. They don't want any nasty surprises later on.

My name was Salmon, like the fish; first name Susie. I was fourteen when I was murdered on December 6, 1973.
– Alice Sebold, opening for *The Lovely Bones*

Add some initial tension to propel the story forward. For a powerful thriller, you need some discord right away, and an "inciting incident" within the first few pages. Jump right in with both feet. Don't rev your engine for too long. On the other hand, I would advise against starting your very first paragraph right in the middle of a critical moment when your hero is already fighting for his life. I think it's best if readers have a chance to get to know him a little first and start getting emotionally invested in him so they'll even care what's happening to him. Some gifted writers are able to successfully start with their protagonist in dire straits, but in general, I'd start just before the proverbial crap hits the fan.

I snapped awake at 2:18 A.M., the bloodshot numerals staring at me from the nightstand. For years on end, I woke up at this exact time every night, regardless of what time zone I was in. But after seventeen years I had just started sleeping through the night. I had finally outrun the old fears. Or so I had convinced myself.
– Greg Hurwitz, opening paragraph of *Trust No One*

So create an intriguing, edgy opening setup that either involves or sets the stage for the inciting incident that smashes the status quo. Devise a situation that causes your protagonist stress, then catapult her world into turmoil. Force her to summon her wits and courage and draw on inner resources to confront impending threats and grapple for solutions. This creates worry, suspense and intrigue, so readers feel compelled to turn the page to find out what happens next.

> It is cold at 6:40 in the morning of a March day in Paris and seems even colder when a man is about to be executed by firing squad.
> – Frederick Forsyth, opening of *Day of the Jackal*

Upset his world. Then, within the first chapter, throw your main character a major curveball. Show something or someone threatening him or people close to him, or other, innocent people. Force your hero to make some difficult, even agonizing decisions. And keep us in his head so we feel his worries or fear or anger or confusion, followed hopefully by strategizing, courage, determination, and actions.

> Some years later, on a tugboat in the Gulf of Mexico, Joe Coughlin's feet were placed in a tub of cement. Twelve gunmen stood waiting until they got far enough out to sea to throw him overboard, while Joe listened to the engine chug and watched the water churn white at the stern. And it occurred to him that almost everything of note that had ever happened in his life—good or bad—had been set in motion the morning he first crossed paths with Emma Gould.
> – Dennis Lehane, first paragraph of *Live by Night*

Make us relate. For maximum reader involvement, introduce a situation of injustice that implicates your protagonist as primary problem-solver. Injustice is something all readers can identify with, and they want to vicariously fight it through a resourceful, courageous, determined hero or heroine.

> The man who wanted to kill the young woman sitting beside me was three-quarters of a mile behind us as we drove through a pastoral setting of tobacco and cotton fields, this humid morning.
> – Jeffery Deaver, first sentence of *Edge*

To recap: So think of a gripping, stressful opening situation for your protagonist that creates empathy and identification for him and raises intriguing story questions. Then show that scene in real time, with tension, action, and dialogue, through the eyes and ears and heart of your protagonist.

> Nat Greco felt like an A cup in a double-D bra.
> – Lisa Scottoline, first line of *Daddy's Girl*

> The night Vincent was shot he saw it coming.
> – Elmore Leonard, first line of *Glitz*

> Cooper Sullivan's life, as he'd known it, was over.
> – Nora Roberts, first line of *Black Hills*

And write tight. Don't rev your engines at the beginning or let your opening sequence drag on. Get in there and be ruthless with your cutting, taking out anything that doesn't drive the story forward or contribute to characterization. Start late and end early.

> A few years ago a psychopath burned down my house.
> – Jonathan Kellerman, first sentence from *Therapy*

That's a tall order, all for a first page. But the business of thriller writing is extremely competitive, so your opening needs to be stellar to stand out in the crowd. Don't waste it with long, meandering descriptive passages about the scenery or weather, or with a character waking up in the morning thinking about his life. This is suspenseful fiction, not literary fiction. And whatever you do, don't use those precious first pages to explain anything to your readers. This is where "show, don't tell" is crucial.

> Jack Reacher ordered espresso, double, no peel, no cube, no foam, no china, and before it arrived at his table he saw a man's life change forever.
> – Lee Child, first line of *The Hard Way*

SOME OTHER TIPS FOR YOUR OPENING SCENE

Your opening scene should be meaningful and relevant to the rest of your story. Don't put your hero in a scene that has nothing to do with the overall plot, just to show readers how tough or determined or charismatic he is. Show him in a scene that directly impacts the rest of the story and leads naturally and organically to the inciting incident, which should happen within the first few pages. In thrillers, every scene needs to count and should contribute in some way to the whole story.

And introduce the antagonist, the villain, soon. One technique that seems to work well for many successful thriller writers is to introduce your protagonist in action in chapter one, then switch to the antagonist's point of view for chapter two, to heighten the tension and fear factor, then back to the hero/heroine for a chapter or two before checking in on the antagonist again. And in the villain's scenes and chapters, it's best to be in his head, in his point of view. So you're using multiple viewpoints, but definitely stay in the protagonist's head more, to keep the readers bonded with him/her. And don't go into the POV of minor characters unless you really need to, and then keep it brief.

SOME NOTES ON STARTING WITH THE VILLAIN

Although I really think it's most effective to start your novel in the viewpoint of your protagonist so readers start bonding with her right away, some thriller writers choose to start with the villain. If you do, I'd keep it brief, maybe just a paragraph or two or a short chapter, then jump to the POV of your protagonist. Readers start identifying with the first person they read about, and they want to identify with the hero, not his nemesis. Also, if you start with the villain, don't portray him in a sympathetic way, as someone we should care about and identify with. This guy tortures and kills innocent people! In the cruelest ways possible. Readers want to fear him, not start sympathizing with him.

Also, I'd keep his actual identity secret from the readers, as well as a lot of details about him, as you don't want readers way ahead of the protagonist, who usually knows nothing about the villain at this point. If the readers know practically everything about him, you risk having them grow impatient with the hero for not discovering all these details more quickly. And it can be boring witnessing the hero figure out things we're already well aware of. Let the readers, for the most part, discover info on the villain along with the hero. That way we have more respect for the hero's resourcefulness and determination, and cheer him/her along more.

Some thriller writers choose to show an opening scene with the villain killing someone. If you do, I'd keep it brief, and it's probably more effective in many ways to show that scene from the point of view of the victim – but spare us every little agonizing detail so early in the book.

Which brings me to another point: Don't start your book with a detailed, in-our-face account of someone being brutally raped or tortured! Or a child being abused. Most readers do not want horrific brutality shoved in their face right in the opening pages! That's just gratuitous violence and is stomach-turning, like seeing photos of tortured animals on Facebook. Remember that readers pick up thrillers to be entertained, not to be disturbed and upset to the core, especially at the very beginning.

TO PROLOGUE OR NOT TO PROLOGUE?

Finally, should you start with a prologue before your chapter one? I strongly advise against it, as many readers skip the prologue and just jump to the actual story. Most readers are eager to get into the story itself – they don't want to feel obligated to read something else first. If you do decide to include a prologue, make it a short, compelling scene in real time, with action and dialogue, in the same tone as the rest of the novel. Don't use it to explain a bunch of stuff to the readers! That's "telling," not "showing" and it's the lazy way out and could turn off a lot of readers, who may then decide not to continue reading.

Resources:
James Scott Bell, *Conflict & Suspense*
James N. Frey, *How to Write a Damn Good Thriller*
Jodie's critical reading and editing of suspense fiction

Chapter 8 – AVOID THESE STORYTELLING GAFFES

BEWARE OF THESE AMATEURISH TYPES OF ERRORS THAT ANNOY READERS

DON'TS FOR YOUR OPENING

These are of course recommendations for success, not hard-and-fast rules.

Don't spend a lot of time revving your engine.

Do skip the prologue and jump right into the story, with your main characters in action, in an intriguing situation with dialogue, interaction, attitude, and tension.

Don't confuse or annoy your readers.

Do situate them right away as to what's going on with the four W's: who, what, where, and when.

Don't begin with a long description of the setting or with background information on your main character.

Do begin with dialogue and action, then add any necessary backstory or description in small doses, on a need-to-know basis as you progress through the story.

Don't start with a character other than your protagonist.

Do introduce your protagonist in the first paragraph, and start right out in his or her point of view. Readers want to know right away whose story it is, which character they should be rooting for.

Don't start with a description of past events.
Do jump right in with what the main character is involved in right now, and introduce some tension or conflict as soon as possible.

Don't start with your character alone, reflecting on his life.
Do have more than one character (two is best) interacting, with action and dialogue. That's more compelling than reading the thoughts of one person.

Don't introduce your protagonist in a static situation.
Do develop your main character quickly by putting her in a bit of hot water and showing how she reacts to the situation, so readers can empathize and "bond" with her, and start caring enough about her to keep reading.

Don't start with everyone happy and things going great – that's just not compelling.
Do start with tension and some conflict, to engage readers right away.

Don't introduce a lot of characters in the first few pages.
Do limit the number of characters you introduce in the first few pages to two or three.

Don't spend too long on setup.
Do show an opening disturbance of some kind on the first page, whether or not it's not the first big confrontation that throws the hero's whole life into turmoil. And make sure the initial incident is meaningful, with consequences directly connected to the overall plot.

Don't wait too long to introduce the villain.
To add tension and intrigue, do show us the antagonist within the first chapter or two.

Don't take chapters to introduce the main conflict or problem the protagonist faces.
Do introduce, within the first chapter, a situation of injustice the

hero has to address. And make the story problem clear to the readers, as well as the hero's story goal.

DON'TS FOR YOUR WHOLE STORY

Avoid these turn-offs anywhere in your novel:

Too much description
Paragraphs of description of the scenery, weather, and other surroundings; also too much detailed information on people and what they're wearing, etc., especially for minor characters.

An unlikeable protagonist
Make sure your main character is someone readers will want to bond with, root for, and follow for the whole story. Don't make him or her cold, arrogant, difficult, demanding, unfeeling, insensitive, dismissive, etc.

A cardboard lead
Make sure your hero or heroine is multidimensional, with personality and attitude, and lots of drive and charisma. Nobody wants to follow a bland, timid, hesitant, needy lead character!

La-la land
Everybody's getting along just fine? No problems? Cause some strife! Why? Because in fiction, happy = boring.

Too much backstory
Don't interrupt the story to give a block of background information on the character – where he grew up, how long he's been at this job, marital history, etc. Weave in only the most relevant or intriguing details, in small bits as you go along, from his point of view, not as the author, and tie it in with what's happening – make it directly relevant to the scene. Flashbacks work well, too, but keep them brief, and again, something in the scene causes the character to start thinking about his past. It doesn't just come out of nowhere.

Omniscient point of view
Avoid interrupting the narrative as the author, addressing the

readers to explain a point or tell them about future or past events, other characters, or something going on somewhere else, all from outside the viewpoint of the character. Keep the readers in the character's head and world at that moment, firmly ensconced in the fictive dream.

Information dumps

Avoid jumping in as the author to explain things to the readers in a lump of exposition. Give them the minimal information they need, still in the character's point of view, with tension and attitude, through searching or a question-and-answer dialogue with someone else. My book, *Fire up Your Fiction*, goes into more detail on this.

AYKB – "As you know, Bob..."

That's a form of info dump through dialogue, where one character is telling another something they both know, just to impart that info to the readers, like "As you know, Bob, we used to live on a farm until we moved to the city when you were ten." Clunky, amateurish and transparent.

Too many similar characters

Make your characters different enough to add contrast, dissonance and sparks.

Characters getting along too well

Even allies such as friends and family members should be interacting with some disagreement and an undercurrent of tension to add interest.

Characters all sound the same – like the author

Make sure each character's dialogue is unique. Their speaking patterns and word choice should reflect their gender, age, background, education, interests, and personality. A rough character isn't going to speak the same way as a professional, and men and women speak quite differently, especially when stressed. This applies to their thoughts as well, of course, and their general internal observations, analysis, and planning.

Chapter 9 – PUT TENSION ON EVERY PAGE

What makes you, as a reader, put down a novel after reading only a few pages or a chapter or two? It's almost always because you're getting bored. Your mind is wandering because the writing lacks sufficient tension. Tension and conflict are the essential elements that drive fiction forward. Unlike in real life, where we strive to avoid stress and resolve conflict, in fiction, a happy scene is always a boring scene. When people are nice to each other and problems get resolved quickly and easily, we yawn and look for another book to sink into.

As Jack M. Bickham says, "In fiction, the best times for the writer – and reader – are when the story's main character is in the worst trouble. Let your character relax, feel happy and content, and be worried about nothing, and your story dies."

Literary agent, writing workshop leader, and writing guru Donald Maass tells us, "Conflict is the magnet that draws reader interest, the discomfort that demands our attention." As Maass counsels aspiring authors, "Without a doubt, the most common flaw I see in manuscripts...is the failure to invest every page of a novel with tension. Low tension equals low interest. High tension equals high interest."

> *"Plot is characters under stress."*
> – Henry James

Every single scene in your novel should have conflict of some kind, whether it's actual arguing and fighting, or just dialogue with an undercurrent of inner doubt, disagreement, disbelief, resentment, indecision, turmoil, or angst. If a scene has no conflict, rewrite it or delete it. Then check to see if you have tension on every single page.

Conflict drives fiction forward because it engages the reader, who has started rooting for the protagonist. Ongoing tension keeps the readers wondering what will happen next, hoping for the best, fearing the worst. As Maass says, "When the conflict level in a novel is high – that is, when it is immediate, credible, personal, unavoidable and urgent – it makes us slow down and read every word. When it is low, we are tempted to skim. We do not care."

"Drama is life with the dull parts left out."
– Alfred Hitchcock

So take out those dull parts – the parts with no conflict or tension, no trouble. And James Scott Bell says, "The greater the trouble, the greater the intensity."

TIPS FOR ADDING TENSION

Start with an inciting incident and bridging conflict.
Today's best-selling novels almost all start with tension and conflict, right from the opening paragraph. This initial tension, the inciting incident, may not – and probably won't – be the main conflict of the story, but it needs to be meaningful and intriguing, in order to draw the reader in long enough to lead to bigger problems the protagonist faces. As Jessica Page Morrell points out, "The inciting incident, the first threat, sets the story in motion and tilts the protagonist off balance."

Donald Maass calls this initial opening tension a "bridging conflict": "There is, in any great opening line, a mini-conflict or tension that is strong enough to carry the reader to the next step in the narrative. [...] After that, another electric spark of tension needs to strike us. If it does not, our interest begins to weaken and will pretty quickly fade out."

So try to hook the reader in right away with a problem or a series of smaller conflicts that serve to capture and keep their attention until the main conflict or first large story question or event appears.

As Maass reveals, "The number one mistake I see in manuscript submissions is a failure to put the main conflict in place quickly enough; or perhaps, a failure to use bridging conflict to keep things going until the main problem is set."

So to hook your readers in, include tension right away in your opening paragraph. Then you'll need to continue to include tension and conflict, whether external (arguments, fights, verbal sparring, threats) or internal (worry, anger, hurt, indecision, fear, angst, frustration, regret) on every page of your novel.

> *"Never duck trouble – conflict – in your story. Seek it out, because that's where excitement and involvement – as well as reader sympathy for your character – lie."*
> – Jack M. Bickham

Give them a protagonist they'll want to worry about.

For readers to invest any interest or concern in the protagonist, they first need to actually care about him. So it's critical to present your main character as a sympathetic, charismatic, resourceful, smart, strong – but vulnerable and conflicted – person the readers will want to root for and start worrying about. And make it clear early on what he really wants or needs. Then start to set up obstacles in his path that force him to reach down deep inside himself to find resources and hidden strengths to overcome them. His ongoing struggles will form your compelling plot and will contribute to his growth as a person, his character arc, making him ultimately stronger, wiser, and even more likeable.

And a worthy villain they'll love to hate.

Make sure your antagonist is multidimensional, clever, determined, and nasty enough that he's worthy of your hero. Give your hero a cunning adversary (or adversaries) who will challenge her to the max, so her struggle to defeat the villain will keep the readers biting their nails and turning the pages.

Write in close third-person POV, or deep point of view.

When readers get right in up close and personal with your character, feeling what she feels, they can't help but be emotionally engaged and on the edge of their seats, worrying about her. Let us see the story world through your protagonist's eyes and other senses, not from some distant omniscient point of view.

Throw the hero into a cauldron.
After your hero or heroine goes through the first door of no return, from the Act I into Act II, they enter the crucible or cauldron, from which there is no escape but to confront the opposition and fight their way out of it. You need to make it obvious why they can't just leave, or the readers will say, "Why don't they just walk away and go home?"

Create real conflict, not just accidents or coincidences.
Jack M. Bickham insists that effective tension in fiction involves conflict between two people, not just random accidents and bad luck for your protagonist. Give your hero or heroine someone they can fight against, to challenge them and help them grow and develop their character and inner strength.

Conflict, according to Bickham, is "active give-and-take, a struggle between story people with opposing goals. It is not, please note, bad luck or adversity. It isn't fate. It's a fight of some kind between people with opposing goals."

Why not just have your character get into an accident? That works well once in a while to throw a wrench in the works, and it will create some sympathy for your character, but in order to really challenge your protagonist and stretch him to his limits, it's usually best to pit him against a foe he can confront in a dramatic way and use his wits and other strengths to defeat. That way he'll be forced to think quickly and use his physical and psychological resources to change the course of events and even avert disaster, which will result in a more exciting plot and a more effective character arc. And it will make the readers bond more with him.

Create complex problems with escalating conflict.
The more complex and challenging the problems your protagonist faces, the more compelling a story it will be for your readers. And as your hero struggles to overcome the odds, raise the stakes even

higher. Show his deepest fears and create obstacles that make him confront and defeat those fears. And it's important that the problems and conflicts the protagonist faces are difficult and complex enough so readers don't see an immediate solution, which would dissipate all the tension.

Also, in terms of fiction technique, Donald Maass specifies, "conflict must undergo complication. It must twist, turn, deepen and grow. Without that constant development, a novel, like a news event, will eventually lose its grip. To break out, simple plot structures need high stakes, complex characters, and layered conflicts."

> *"In breakout fiction, the central conflict is as deep and as bad as it can possibly be."*
> – Donald Maass

Maass spells out in detail the kind of ongoing, deepening tension needed for creating a page-turner, a breakout novel: "Conflict that holds our attention for long periods of time is meaningful, immediate, large-scale, surprising, not easily resolved, and happens to people for whom we feel sympathy."

On the other hand, "Problems that are abstract, remote, trivial, ordinary, easily overcome, and/or happening to someone for whom we feel little...cannot fuel a gripping novel."

Create subtle or overt tension, resentments, or competition even among friends, family members, co-workers, or allies.
Even in scenes where friends, neighbors, siblings, relatives, or colleagues are interacting, include some subtle discord, jealousies, resentments, competitiveness or other emotional friction. Think of that great old pop psychology book, *Games People Play*, by Eric Berne, and avoid the reasonable, mature, cheery adult-adult interaction in favor of the tenser "parent-child" combinations, like having one sibling or friend give the other unwanted advice, all in the guise of "helping."

Include sexual or romantic tension to spice things up.
For variety or to further the plot, consider adding in some romantic

or sexual tension between the protagonist and another important character. Create social or work barriers to the relationship (think Romeo and Juliette) or use obstacles, circumstances, attitudes, or distance to keep them apart when they may be fighting it, but they're obviously drawn together.

All dialogue needs tension, too.

As Ingermanson and Economy say, "Dialogue is war! Every dialogue should be a controlled conflict between at least two of the characters with opposing agendas. The main purpose of dialogue is to advance the conflict of the story." So definitely leave out the "How are you? I'm fine. And you?" yadda, yadda, and cut to the chase. Unless of course you're trying to show seething resentment or subtle tension boiling up from under surface politeness. In that case, show that undercurrent of tension. We should see the POV character's doubt or disbelief or disagreement with what the other person is saying, whether it's overtly expressed or not. Show the power struggles, the ego and personality clashes, the main character's anger or disdain or inner conflict, either overtly or subtly.

Throw in some pressures and time constraints.

Maybe your heroine is late for work or an important appointment, date, or interview. Get the old clock – or bomb – ticking. A car drives up as your hero is searching a house for clues. Or maybe the kidnappers' deadline is fast approaching.

Plan some kind of change, reversal, or surprise for every scene.

The character's plans, opinions or feelings change; circumstances change; the outcome takes an unexpected turn.

Throw in some hyper-suspense.

According to James Scott Bell, "Hyper-suspense happens when the character does not know what the forces are that oppose him – and neither does the reader." This works especially well with first-person narration, or limited third-person, where readers don't get into the head of the antagonist. In fact, we don't know anything the protagonist doesn't know. We're creeping along with him, looking around, trying to figure out what's happening at every turn.

Add obstacles and complications.
The hero's plans get thwarted; his gun jams or falls into a river during a scuffle; he's stuck in traffic on a bridge; her car breaks down; he's kicked off the case; her cell phone battery dies just when she needs it most; the power goes out, leaving the room in total darkness; a truck blocks the only way out of the alley – you get the picture. Think Jack Reacher, Lucy Kincaid, Elvis Cole, Eve Dallas, Joe Pike, Maggie O'Dell, Harry Bosch, or Stephanie Plum in any number of escapades. The character has to find inner resources to discover a way around each new obstacle or out of each new dilemma.

Create critical turning points or dilemmas as you go along.
Which way did the bad guys go? Should she open that door or not? Who to believe? Go up the stairs or down? Turn right or left? Answer the phone or let it ring?

Incapacitate your hero.
Your heroine is given a drug that makes her dizzy and hallucinating; your hero breaks his leg and can't escape or give chase; she's bound and gagged; he's blinded by sand in his eyes...

Show your protagonist's anxiety, inner fears, and insecurities.
Also, show rapidly changing emotions – vague unease turns to fear, which escalates to terror.

Vary the level of tension – write in highs and lows.
Of course, it's not necessary or even desirable to show nonstop edge-of-your-seat high-tension conflict – that would wear your readers out. But, as mentioned earlier, even in relatively quiet scenes, show the inner tension of your character – worry, fear, anger, confusion – and dissonance with others.

As James Scott Bell says, "You want to have some sort of tension in every scene, though it doesn't have to be of the highest sort. That would wear out the reader. [...] ...give your readers some breathing room, too. But when they breathe, let it be with a tight chest."

CONCLUSION

So, why do we need lots of tension and conflict in a page-turner?

• Readers bond much more quickly to a character who is conflicted, worried, frustrated, or facing any kind of adversity.

• Ongoing tension and conflict heighten and sustain readers' involvement and keep them turning the pages.

• High tension and conflict bring to the surface readers' deepest anxieties. When, through the protagonist, they vicariously face them and defeat them, this creates feelings of belonging, relief, accomplishment, and satisfaction.

So if you want to write a novel that sells, remember Donald Maass's words of wisdom:

> *"Tension on every page is a technique that keeps readers glued to a novel.... It is a key breakout skill."*

Resources:

James Scott Bell, *Revision and Self-Editing*
Jack M. Bickham, *The 38 Most Common Fiction Writing Mistakes (And How to Avoid Them)*
Donald Maass, *Writing the Breakout Novel*
Jessica Page Morrell, *Thanks, But This Isn't For Us*

Chapter 10 – WRITE RIVETING SCENES AND CHAPTERS

Do you have a scene in your novel where nothing much really happens, where your protagonist isn't in trouble, or at least challenged? Where there's not a lot of tension and no major developments or setbacks? If so, rewrite that scene or take it out, with any essential bits from it inserted somewhere else. If you leave it as is, that could well be the scene where your readers decide the story is lagging, and they put it down – and don't pick it up again.

There's no place for "filler" in a page-turning thriller. Today's readers are much more impatient than readers of the past, much less willing to slog on through boring parts to see if things improve. Every scene needs to grab them with lots of tension and intrigue. Anything significant needs to be "shown," not "told" (see Chapter 12, "Show, Don't Tell"), and the events and dialogue of every scene need to move the plot along and result in a significant change in the characters and their situation.

EVERY SCENE NEEDS TENSION AND A CHANGE

Every scene needs tension.

As James Scott Bell says, "Every scene in your novel should have tension, whether that comes from outright conflict or the inner turmoil of character emotions." How do you create that needed conflict? According to Bell, "You create outer tension by giving the POV character a scene objective. What does he want, and why? It has to matter to him, or it won't to us."

Then decide what kinds of obstacles should keep your protagonist from reaching his goal. It could be another character (or several) with an opposing agenda, or a difficult circumstance, or both.
Finally, to continue the tension flowing into the next scene, and to keep the reader worried and reading, it's best to make most scenes come out with the character suffering a setback.

Of course, not every scene is going to have a fight or a screaming match. But even in quieter scenes, it's important to show the inner tension of your viewpoint character – worry, concern, irritability, anxiety, doubt, indecision. Also show the tension of other characters by their words, actions, tone of voice, facial expressions and body language.

Each scene needs significant change.

As Hallie Ephron says, "In the course of each scene, some change should occur to move your story forward. It's not enough for a scene to just introduce a character or convey lots of fascinating information about the setting. In every scene, something has to change. This means that something has to happen that changes the situation, or a character's perception of it, and that change propels the story forward."

The change that occurs in a scene can be a shift in a character's emotional state, their relationship with others, or their situation – usually for the worst. And the change needs to result in character growth or plot change.

Write tight, compelling scenes. Start late and end early.

Besides making sure every scene has conflict and change, and events are "shown," not described or "told," another tip for keeping your readers turning the pages is to start each scene as late as possible. In other words, don't spend a lot of time with description and setup – start just as things are getting rolling.

However, it's important to remember that even though you want to start late, don't forget to orient the reader at the start of each scene by establishing right away who the viewpoint character is for the scene and when and where the action is taking place. This brief setting of the scene should happen within the first sentence or two, to avoid reader confusion and frustration.

Secondly, end each scene and chapter as early as possible. Don't let scenes dribble off – instead, end each scene on a powerful note that propels the readers forward with a new story question for the next scene or chapter. Resist the urge to say the same thing in several ways or to add more minor details. And don't resolve everything at the end of the scene – leave readers hanging most of the time, with your protagonist still struggling.

A blueprint for writing strong scenes:

Jack M. Bickham gives us some specific advice for writing powerful scenes. According to him, any time you start to write a scene, you should go through the following process (reworded slightly for brevity, and my italics):

1. Decide specifically what the main character's *immediate goal* is.
2. Get this written down clearly in the copy.
3. On a separate note to yourself, write down, clearly and briefly, what the *scene question* is. Word it so it can be answered by "yes" or "no."
4. In your story, after the goal has been shown, bring in another character who now states, just as clearly, his *opposition*.
5. Plan all the maneuvers and steps in the *conflict* between the two characters you have set up.
6. Write the scene moment-by-moment; no summary.
7. Devise a *disastrous ending* of the scene – a turning of the tables or surprise that *answers the scene question* badly." [ends badly for the protagonist]

Bickham concludes, "Please note, however, that none of this can happen – nothing can work – if the scene does not grab your readers and intensely involve them. To accomplish that, the scene must be lifelike."

So don't tell us what happened – show the action in real time, with plenty of tension, revealing throughout the scene the viewpoint character's goals, emotions, reactions, and sensory perceptions.

Writing high-tension scenes

Your plot should include a few especially tense scenes, probably one in the middle, and the biggest one for the climax, where the tension, conflict, suspense and action are at an extreme level.

To design these pivotal scenes or "set pieces," as they call them in screenwriting, you'll need to brainstorm for the worst thing that can happen to your protagonist at that time. Make a list and pick the scariest possibility.

Once you've decided what will happen in that scene, maximize the tension by building up to it and hinting at it beforehand, to raise the apprehension of the readers. Set up the danger ahead of time for the readers, by making it something the protagonist or someone close to them is worried might happen, or a glimpse we see into the villain's plans, etc.

And once you're in the scene, be sure to show us how your character is feeling. Make the readers aware of their doubts, anxieties, fears, and determination. Show their decision-making process, so we're right there with them, trying to figure a way out of the dilemma or how to stop the destructive plans of the bad guy. And give us the details of how they're feeling physically as well. Perhaps they're injured and in pain. Or showing physical signs of terror or panicking.

Resources:
James Scott Bell, *Revision and Self-Editing*
Jack M. Bickham, *The 38 Most Common Fiction Writing Mistakes (And How to Avoid Them)*
Hallie Ephron, *The Everything Guide to Writing Your First Novel*
Jessica Page Morrell, *Between the Lines*

PART V

BRING YOUR CHARACTERS TO LIFE ON THE PAGE

Chapter 11 – POWERFUL POINT OF VIEW

USE DEEP POINT OF VIEW

To suck your readers into your story world and keep them turning the pages, write your story in deep point of view, or close third person (or first person). Get us up close and personal with your protagonist and show us her inner reactions, fears, hopes, dreams, and regrets, as well as how she's feeling physically at moments of stress.

When we experience the story through her eyes and other senses, reacting as she does to her problems, it sucks us into her psyche and her situation. It's like we almost become her, and we're compelled to keep reading, hoping everything will turn out right.

When we stick mainly with our protagonist, in his head and heart, with a bare minimum or no stepping back to describe things from the author's stance (omniscient POV), we're using deep point of view, or close third, which is a lot like first-person point of view, with the added freedom of switching to the villain's or some other character's POV when it suits our purpose. Deep POV is a powerful way of drawing readers into your story quickly and making them worry about your hero right away, and keep worrying – which is exactly what you want!

But how do you go about this? Let's suppose you're writing a story about a macho, hero-type guy named Kurt, who defeats the villain, restores justice, and even gets the girl. It's Kurt's story so he's your main viewpoint character. How do you make sure your handling of his viewpoint is as powerful as it can possibly be?

The first thing you need to do is imagine the setting, people, and events not as you see them, but as they would be perceived by Kurt, and only by him. As you write the chapters where Kurt is the POV character (which should be at least 70% of the whole book), you the writer must become Kurt. You see what he sees, and nothing more. You know what he knows, and nothing more. When Kurt walks into a bar, you do not imagine how the bar looks from some god-like authorial stance high above, or as a movie camera might see it; you see it only as Kurt sees it, walking in purposefully and looking around.

And of course include his reactions to the other people in the bar. Show Kurt's feelings (and only his) about what and who he's seeing, and his reactions to the situation. Instead of saying, "The bar was noisy, dark and smoky," say "The cigarette smoke in the air stung Kurt's eyes and, in the dim light, he couldn't make out if his target was there. As he looked around, the room started to quiet down. Heads turned, and eyes took him in, some curious, some hostile." This way, the reader is seeing the scene through Kurt's head and identifying with him, starting to worry about him. This from-the-inside-out approach is vital if you want your reader to care about your protagonist and get truly engaged in your story.

But you need to go even further – you need to describe what he's seeing and feeling, his internal reactions to what's around him, by using only words and expressions that he would use. If your character is a rancher or a drifter or a hard-boiled P.I, or a young child, you're not going to describe the scene or his reactions in highly educated, articulate, flowery terms, or tell about things he probably wouldn't notice, like the color-coordination of the décor, the chandeliers, or the arrangement of dried flowers in an urn on the floor.

It's also important to be vigilant that your viewpoint doesn't slip, and you're suddenly giving someone else's opinion about Kurt, or telling about something that's happening out in the street or even in a hidden corner of the bar, while Kurt is still at the entrance of the bar. Let the reader know other people's reactions to Kurt, not by going into those characters' heads at this point, but by what Kurt perceives—he sees their disapproving, admiring, angry, curious, or intense looks, picks up on their body language, hears their words and tone of voice, sees them get up and stride toward him or head out the back way or whatever.

Then, in a later scene or chapter, you can go into the bad guy's point of view and find out what he thinks of Kurt. Or, once he meets the girl, write a scene or chapter in her viewpoint so the reader finds out more about her and what she thinks of our hero Kurt.

This technique, properly used, will suck your readers effectively into your story world, where they really want to be, engaged, involved, and connected.

USE MULTIPLE VIEWPOINTS

Consider occasionally inserting a scene or chapter in the villain's point of view, for added depth, tension, and suspense.

Or, in a romantic suspense, like Sandra Brown, Nora Roberts, and many other talented authors write, where you're mainly in the viewpoint of your female lead, insert some scenes in the POV of her love interest, partner, or adversary with chemistry developing.

If you really like first person for your protagonist but also want to get into the head of the antagonist, be sure to use third person for the villain. Having his sections also in first person ("I") would be just too confusing! And irritating, as at the start of the chapter, readers would assume "I" is the hero or heroine, and would then have to adjust their thinking.

Chapter 12 – SHOW, DON'T TELL

"Show, don't tell" is the most common mantra among advisors to fiction writers. It's about bringing the scene alive and putting the reader right there, inside your character, experiencing her fear along with her, feeling the sweat on his brow and his adrenaline racing, our pulse quickening right along with theirs, muscles tensed, ready to leap into action.

A common mistake among aspiring fiction writers is to describe or narrate (tell) events as if they took place at some point in the past, instead of putting the reader right in the middle of the action and showing the events as they occur, in real time, along with the characters' reactions, feelings, and actual words (direct dialogue).

To clarify what is meant by "show, don't tell," think of it this way: Which would you rather do, go see a great movie in a theatre with a big screen and surround sound ("show"), maybe even in 3D, or hear about the movie from someone else afterward ("tell")? That's the difference we're talking about here.

According to Ingermanson and Economy, "Showing means presenting the story to the reader using sensory information. The reader wants to see the story, hear it, smell it, feel it, and taste it, all the while experiencing the thoughts and feelings of a living, breathing character. Telling means summarizing the story for the reader in a way that skips past the sensory information and goes straight to the facts."

Janet Evanovich considers "show, don't tell" to be one of the most important principles of fiction: "Instead of stating a situation flat out, you want to let the reader discover what you're trying to say by watching a character in action and by listening to his dialogue. Showing brings your characters to life."

Showing also makes your readers feel more involved, like an active partner in the process. As Jack Bickham says, "Not only does moment-by-moment development make the scene seem most lifelike, it's in a scene [with dialogue and action and reaction] where your reader gets most of his excitement. If you summarize, your reader will feel cheated – short-changed of what he reads for – without quite knowing why."

Lisa Jackson, in *Something Wicked*, could have told us:

> Savannah woke up to find herself tied up on top of a kitchen island.

Instead, she showed us the scene with vivid detail, including Savannah's thoughts and physical sensations:

> Savannah's first conscious thought was that she was lying on a cold slab. Every muscle ached, and she was freezing. She slowly came awake to realize she was lying naked atop a granite kitchen island. Bluish moonlight left a hard rectangle across her feet, the only illumination in an otherwise dark room.
>
> She tried to lift her hand, but it was tied down. Both hands were. And her legs.
>
> "Been waiting for you...," a voice said silkily from across the room.

Harlan Coben, in his gripping thriller, *Tell No One*, could have said:

> "I was scared."

Instead, he said:

> "Fear wrapped itself around my chest like steel bands."

Of course, you can't show everything, or your book would be way too long and would tire your readers out – or worse, end up boring them. Reserve the showing for important scenes. Basically, the more intense the moment, the more showing you should do. You don't want to describe every move your characters make at down times, or when going from one place to the other. That's where you summarize or "tell," to get them to the next important scene quickly, without a lot of boring detail.

The main thing to keep in mind is to never to tell the reader, after the fact (or have a character telling another character), about a critical scene. Instead, dramatize it in the here and now, with dialogue, action, and lots of sensory details to bring it to life for the reader.

Use sensory imagery – evoke all five senses.
Don't just show us what the character is seeing – we need to know what she is hearing, smelling, touching, tasting, and also tactile sensations on her skin, like sweating or cold, clammy skin. Also show us what's going on inside her body, like heart palpating, difficulty breathing, tight chest, roiling stomach, nausea, etc.

Show your character's thoughts, feelings, and reactions.
Bring your character to life and make the readers bond with him and worry about him by showing his inner thoughts and reactions. Here's a before-and-after example, disguised from my editing:

Before:

"What do you mean *them*? Who else are you talking about?"

"The others who've been killed," Tim said. "That's who."

"*Killed*? What are you talking about?"

"Just what I said," Tim replied. "Killed. Friggin murdered, man. At least three of them in the past month."

"I don't understand," Keith said as he looked around at the room.

Jodie's comments to the author: This is kind of bland. I would think he'd be very confused and worried – freaked out. Show his reaction and feelings here.

After:

"What do you mean *them*? Who else are you talking about?"

"The others who've been killed," Tim said. "That's who."

"*Killed*? What the hell are you talking about?"

"Just what I said," Tim replied. "Killed. Friggin murdered, man. At least three of them in the past month."

Keith's eyes widened as the words reverberated in his mind. *Killed? Murdered? Is this guy serious?* "I don't understand." He got up, ran his hands through his hair, and started pacing around the room. *What the hell is going on?*

Show your character's immediate internal reactions.
An effective trick is to show how your character is reacting by a quick, internal direct thought, usually expressed in italics, like *What? No way!*

In *Dirty Blonde*, Lisa Scottoline's protagonist, Cate, reacts internally and immediately a lot, which is very effective in showing us how she's feeling about what's happening. I like the way Scottoline sprinkles in brief internal reactions in italics, at the beginnings of paragraphs, like: *Oh, God.* Or *Argh.* Or *Jerk.* Or *Great.* Or *Rats. I mean thanks.*

In *Mystic River*, Dennis Lehane shows us the POV character Jimmy's regrets and self-loathing:

Setup: He's just gotten off the phone telling his wife their daughter Katie's car has been found and police are searching the park for her, and it doesn't look good. His wife, Annabeth, is almost hysterical and incredulous, asking him why the hell he's standing out on the street, idle, instead of in the park searching for his daughter.

"Get in there, Jimmy. I mean, God, what's wrong with you?"

She hung up.

Jimmy handed the phone back to Chuck, knowing that Annabeth was right. She was so completely right that it killed Jimmy to realize that he would regret his impotence of the last forty-five minutes for the rest of his life, never be able to think about it without cringing, trying to crawl away from it in his head. When had he become this thing—this man who'd say yes, sir, no, sir, right you are, sir, to fucking cops when his firstborn daughter was missing? When had that happened? When had he stood at a counter and handed his dick over in exchange for feeling like, what, an upright citizen?

You can't help feeling Jimmy's pain and remorse and self-loathing here. Without these inner thoughts and feelings, this scene would lack so much depth. Not only that, this really adds to Jimmy's characterization and our sympathy for him, and helps us bond with him more, as we feel his pain and guilt.

PART VI

SUSTAIN THE SUSPENSE

Chapter 13 – BUILD IN TENSION & INTRIGUE

Build suspense and apprehension from your very first paragraph.

All genres of fiction, not just thrillers and action-adventures, need tension, suspense, and intrigue to keep the reader invested in finishing your story. And of course, you'll need to ratchet up the uneasiness and anticipation a lot more if you're writing a fast-paced, nail-biting page-turner.

New York literary agent Noah Lukeman, author of *The Plot Thickens* and other great craft books, says that if a writer can maintain suspense throughout the story, many readers will keep reading even if the characters are undeveloped and the plot is weak. So learning to write suspenseful fiction is definitely a ticket to increased sales.

Suspenseful writing makes the readers feel curious, concerned, anxious. They start to worry about what's going to happen to the protagonist, and this unease and concern keep them turning the pages.

What is suspense, anyway? Alfred Hitchcock, a master at suspense, was once asked to define the term. He told the interviewer to imagine two people sitting at a table at a café. Under the table is a bag. In the bag is a bomb. The characters don't know that the bomb is there, but the viewers do. That, he said, is suspense.

And as Steven James explained in his excellent workshop at

Thrillerfest 2011, "Suspense needs apprehension. Apprehension is suspense. And impending danger creates apprehension." James points out that suspense is about first making a promise (setting reader expectations that your characters and story are going to intrigue them) and then providing a payoff. "The bigger the promise, the bigger the payoff," says James. "Give the reader what he wants or something better."

Ian Irvine tells us that holding back critical information creates suspense: "Suspense comes from readers' anticipation of what's going to come next. Therefore, never tell your readers anything in advance when, by withholding it, you can increase suspense."

How do we write suspenseful, page-turning scenes?

Create a complex character that readers will worry about, then write an opening that grabs the reader's curiosity right away, with an intriguing story question, a worrisome undercurrent, and an inciting incident.

Then follow this up for most of the story with hints of even worse trouble to come. Add in some foreshadowing here and there, in small doses, to keep the readers off-balance, wondering and worrying. Delay revealing critical information, either about the protagonist or the antagonist, and build slowly.

Drop little hints as you go along of deep hidden secrets in the protagonist's past that could trip him up, or new developments in the villain's plans, or other perils to come. Resist the urge to reveal too much too soon. These hints and delays are what create suspense. As Jessica Morrell says, "Suspense builds and satisfies when the reader desperately wants something to happen and it isn't happening."

Suspense is about exploiting the readers' insecurities and basic fears of the unknown, their inner need to vicariously vanquish foes, thwart evil, and win over adversity. For heightened suspense, use deep point of view, so the readers are right there in your protagonist's head, privy to her fears and insecurities, struggling with her against her adversaries and other dire threats.

So build the suspense gradually, teasing the reader with possibilities, and keep it escalating, with the occasional short breather, then throw in setbacks or new challenges. Repeat as needed throughout the book, always providing a brief reprieve between these tense, nerve-wracking scenes.

SOME "BIG-PICTURE" TECHNIQUES FOR ADDING SUSPENSE

First, make your readers care about your protagonist.
If readers haven't bonded with your main character, they won't become emotionally invested in what happens to him or her. As William Bernhardt says, "If people don't care about your characters, nothing else matters."

Create a cunning, frightening villain.
Your villain needs to be as clever, determined and resourceful as your protagonist – or even more so. Make him a serious force to be reckoned with!

Threaten your protagonist.
Now that your readers care about your main character, insert a major threat or dilemma within the first chapter. Create an over-riding sentence about this to keep in mind as you're writing your story: Will (name) survive/stop/find/overcome (difficulty/threat)? This is your main story question that sets up the macro suspense of your whole novel, and isn't answered until the end.

But don't pull out all of the stops on the first page.
When writing suspense, start slowly and subtly – give yourself somewhere to build. As Hallie Ephron says, "If you pull out all the stops at the beginning, you'll have nowhere to go; worse still, your reader will turn numb to the nuance you are trying to create."

Establish urgency, a tense mood, and generally fast pacing.
Unlike cozy mysteries and other more leisurely genres, thrillers and other suspense fiction generally need a tense mood and fast pacing throughout most of the novel, with short "breathers" in between the tensest scenes.

Use multiple viewpoints, especially that of the villain.

For increased anxiety and suspense, get us into the head of your antagonist from time to time. This way the readers find out critical information the heroine doesn't know, things we want to warn her about! And getting into the head of the bad guy always enriches the story, even if we don't know his identity yet – he's just a scary shadowy character with diabolical thoughts and plans.

Keep the story momentum moving forward.

Don't get bogged down in backstory or exposition. Keep the action moving ahead, especially in the first chapter. Then add in background and other info little by little, on an "as-needed" basis only.

Create a mood of unease.

Keep the readers on edge by showing the main character feeling apprehensive about something or someone or revealing some of the bad guy's thoughts and intentions.

Or maybe, instead of anxious, your heroine is oblivious, but because we've just been in the viewpoint of the villain, we know the danger that's about to threaten her. Create anxiety in the reader and keep ratcheting it up.

Add in tough choices and moral dilemmas.

Devise ongoing difficult decisions and inner conflict for your lead character. These will not only make your plot more suspenseful, they will also make your protagonist more complex, vulnerable, and interesting.

Withhold information.

Don't tell your readers too much too soon. Dole out information little by little, to tantalize readers and keep them wondering. Keep details of the past of both your protagonist and antagonist hidden, and hint at critical, life-altering experiences they've had that are impacting their present goals, desires, fears, etc. Add one significant detail after another as you go along.

Delay answers to critical plot questions.

Look for places in your story where you've answered readers' questions too soon, so have missed a prime spot to increase tension and suspense. Draw out the time before answering that question. In the meantime, hint at it to remind readers of its importance.

Use dramatic irony.
This is where your readers know something critical and scary that the protagonist is not aware of. For example, your heroine is relaxing after a stressful day, unaware that the killer is prying open her basement window. Or your hero is approaching his vehicle, unaware that it's been rigged with a bomb that is set to go off when he turns the key in the ignition.

Add a ticking clock.
Adding time pressure is another excellent way to increase suspense. Lee Child is a master at this, a great example being his thriller *61 Hours*. Or how about those great MacGyver shows, where he had to devise ways to defuse the bomb before it exploded and killed all kinds of innocent people? Or the TV series *24*, with agent Jack Bauer?

Use the setting to establish the mood and create suspense.
This is the equivalent of ominous music, harsh lighting, strange camera angles, or nasty weather in a scary movie. To describe the surroundings of the character in jeopardy, use strong descriptors, vivid details, and evocative sensory imagery that reflect or add to his angst or fears and bring to life the dangerous situations he's confronting. This applies to both indoor and outdoor settings, of course.

Use compelling, vivid sensory imagery to take us right there, with the protagonist, vividly experiencing and reacting to whoever/whatever is challenging or threatening her.

Appeal to all five senses, not just the visual.
Show breaking glass, a dripping faucet, footsteps on the stairs, a crash in the basement, rumbling of thunder, a sudden cold draft, an animal brushing the skin in the dark, a freezing cold, blinding blizzard, a putrid smell coming from the basement...

Show, don't tell.
Show all your critical scenes in real time, with action, reaction, and

dialogue. Show your character's inner feelings and physical and emotional reactions. Don't have one character tell another about an important event or scene.

What the reader desperately wants to happen isn't happening – yet.
Promise change but delay it.

Put some suspense in every scene.
There should be something unresolved in every scene. Your character enters the scene with an objective and encounters obstacles in the scene, so she is unable to reach her goals.

Vary the tension.
But of course, you can't keep up tension nonstop, as it's tiring for readers and will eventually numb them. It's best to intersperse tense, nail-biting scenes with a few more leisurely, relaxed scenes that provide a bit of reprieve before the next tense, harrowing scene starts.

Use brief flashbacks.
At key moments, reveal your main character's childhood traumas, unpleasant events, secrets, emotional baggage, hangups, dysfunctional family, etc.

Keep raising the stakes.
Keep asking yourself, "How can I make things worse for the protagonist?" As the challenges get more difficult and the obstacles more insurmountable, readers worry more and more about whether he can beat the ever-increasing odds against him, and suspense grows.

And as a bonus, as William Bernhardt says, "increasing pressure leads to increasing insight into the character." Which leads to increased reader engagement.

Plan a few plot twists.
Readers are surprised and delighted when the events take a turn they never expected. Don't let your readers become complacent, thinking it's easy to figure out the ending, or they may stop reading.

Vary your sentence structure to mirror the action and mood.
Longer sentences suit a more leisurely pace and shorter sentences and sentence fragments are usually better at times of high tension.

Resources:
James Scott Bell, *Conflict & Suspense*
William Bernhardt, Thrillerfest workshop
Jack M. Bickham, *The 38 Most Common Fiction Writing Mistakes*
Hallie Ephron, *The Everything Guide to Writing Your First Novel*
Ian Irvine, ian-irvine.com
Steven James, Workshop, Craftfest, 2011
Jessica Page Morrell, *Between the Lines*

Chapter 14 – USE FORESHADOWING FOR MAXIMUM READER INVOLVEMENT

DEVICES FOR AMPING UP THE TENSION AND SUSPENSE

Throughout your novel, you want to continually provoke reader curiosity and apprehension, so they keep anxiously turning the pages. Here are some specific devices that add tension, suspense, and intrigue to your story:

• Foreshadowing
• Withholding information, delaying
• Secrets
• Stretching out the tension
• Epiphanies and revelations

In this chapter, we'll cover foreshadowing, an indispensable literary device for adding suspense, and one that requires planning, implementation, and a bit of expertise to really be effective.

FORESHADOWING

Foreshadowing is about dropping little clues about possible secrets, revelations, complications, and trouble to come. To pique the reader's interest and keep her reading, hint at dangers lurking ahead. Foreshadowing incites curiosity, anticipation, and worry in the readers, and also prepares them somewhat for the possibility of later occurrences, so lends some credibility when the hinted-at event does occur.

For example, in the opening of *The Wizard of Oz*, when Dorothy's still in Kansas, the transformation of Miss Gulch into a witch on a broomstick foreshadows her reappearance as Dorothy's enemy in Oz.

But be subtle about it. If you make it obvious, it takes away the suspense and intrigue, along with the reader's pleasure at trying to figure everything out.

As Lynn Franklin says, "This does not mean that you are going to give away the ending. Think of foreshadowing as setup. The best foreshadowing is subtle and is woven into the story – often in multiple ways. In this fashion, foreshadowing helps build tension and gives resonance and power to the story."

Why is foreshadowing important?

Foreshadowing is a way of alerting readers to the possibility of upcoming critical events, of telling them to keep reading because some exciting developments are ahead.

Foreshadowing creates suspense. According to the dictionary, suspense is "a quality in a work of fiction that arouses excited expectation about what may happen."

If you don't foreshadow events and developments to come, readers will have no expectations, so no anticipation. Foreshadowing stimulates curiosity and provides intrigue, increasing tension and suspense.

Also, if events and changes are foreshadowed, when they do occur, they seem more credible, not just a random act or something you suddenly decided to stick in there, especially if they're unexpected. For example, if your forty-something, somewhat bumbling detective suddenly starts using Taekwondo to defeat his opponent, you'd better have mentioned at some point earlier that he takes or has taken Taekwondo lessons, or else the readers are going to say, "Oh, come on! Give me a break."

Well-known nineteenth-century Russian author Anton Chekhov once said in a letter to another author, "One must not put a loaded rifle on the stage if no one is thinking of firing it." (*Letter to Aleksandr Semenovich Lazarev, November 1889.*) So, according to Chekhov, if you drop hints or create a subtle "alert" to an object or a piece of information, you must, at some point, follow up by delivering the payoff – the gun that we were made aware of earlier eventually gets fired. Of course, you could always put a spin on it, creating a great twist. For example, the gun gets used, but not in the way you expected it to be used. Perhaps, instead of the character shooting someone or getting shot with it, he uses it to commit suicide, or someone steals it and uses it elsewhere. You're still keeping your promise to the readers and maintaining their trust, but you've also added the bonus of a surprise twist.

Dropping little hints ahead of your critical, high-tension scenes increases their plausibility, impact, and potency by providing some necessary build-up to them.

How to use foreshadowing:

Use foreshadowing to lay the groundwork for future tension, to tantalize readers about upcoming critical scenes, confrontations or developments, major changes or reversals, character transformations, or secrets to be revealed.

Foreshadowing to add worry and reader engagement

Early thoughts, reactions, and actions in a character, as well as revelations about them, build characterization and give us clues to their vulnerabilities, fears, and secrets, so this kind of foreshadowing lays the groundwork for other events and makes readers anxious about them.

Early hints or indications of character flaws, phobias, or weaknesses make the readers concerned about how they'll deal with adversity later. If we find out early on that your character has a fear of heights, then when she has to scale a cliff, we'll really worry about her. And worried readers are emotionally engaged readers, which is exactly what you want. For example, in Andrew E. Kaufman's psychological thriller *The Lion, The Lamb, The Hunted*, we find out fairly early on that Patrick, the protagonist, is a bleeder. So of course whenever he's in any kind of physical confrontation or danger, especially if he's nowhere near a hospital or clinic, we worry about him bleeding to death. So what happens partway through the story? He gets bitten by a dog – in an isolated area!

Foreshadowing to reveal character traits and build character motivations

Foreshadowing is a great way to show and build character motivations so their later decisions and actions seem plausible. For example, a teenager who jumps in to help an accident victim by calmly assuring the patient, stopping the blood flow with a tourniquet, and splinting a fracture with a branch and a torn shirt may seem very unlikely, but if you reveal earlier that she wants to be a doctor and has taken First Aid courses, her actions are now quite believable.

And foreshadowing is also very effective in revealing the motivations of your antagonist. A typical way to reveal characteristics and motivation of your villain is, when you're in their point of view, having them recall moments of their youth when they were treated unfairly or abused or when they picked on younger children or tortured birds or animals.

Some ideas for foreshadowing:

Here are some of the ways you can foreshadow events or revelations in your story:

• Show a pre-scene or mini-example of what happens in a big way later:

The roads are icy and the car starts to skid but the driver manages to get it under control and continues driving, a little shaken and nervous. This initial near-miss plants worry in the reader's mind. Then later a truck comes barreling toward him and... (or the icy road causes some other kind of accident).

• The protagonist overhears snippets of conversation or gossip and tries to piece it all together, but it doesn't all make sense until later.

• Hint at shameful secrets or bad memories your protagonist has been hiding, trying to forget about.

• Something on the news warns of possible danger – a storm brewing, a convict who's escaped from prison, a killer on the loose, a series of bank robberies, etc.

• Your main character notices and wonders about other characters' unusual or suspicious actions, reactions, tone of voice, facial expressions, or body language. Another character, perhaps a spouse or loved one, acts evasive or looks preoccupied, nervous, apprehensive, or tense.

• Show us the protagonist's inner fears or suspicions. Then the readers start worrying that what the character is anxious about may happen.

• Use setting details and word choices to create an ominous mood. A storm is brewing, or fog or a snowstorm makes it impossible to see any distance ahead, or...?

• The protagonist or a loved one has a disturbing dream or premonition.

• A fortune teller or horoscope foretells trouble ahead.

• Based on past experiences, the character forms an opinion about something that could happen.

• Use objects: your character is looking for something in a drawer and pushes aside a loaded gun. Or a knife, scissors, or other dangerous object or poisonous substance is lying around within reach of children or an assailant.

• Make the ordinary seem ominous, or plant something out of place in a scene. Zoom in on an otherwise benign object, like that bicycle lying in the sidewalk, the half-empty glass on the previously spotless kitchen counter, or the single child's shoe in the alley, to create a sense of unease. Or something is slightly off, just enough to create a niggling doubt in the mind of the reader. A phone off the hook, an open window, wet footprints on the floor, a book or notepad on the floor, a half-eaten breakfast, etc.

• Use symbolism, like a broken mirror, a dead bird, a lost kitten, or, as in Hemingway's foreshadowing of an early death in the opening line of his *A Farewell to Arms*:

The leaves fell early that year.

A no-no about foreshadowing:

But don't step in as the author giving an aside to the readers, like "When she woke up that morning, she had no idea it would turn out to be the worst day of her life." The author should stay out of the book, not jump in and address the readers. We're in the heroine's head at that moment, and since she has no idea how the day is going to turn out, it's breaking the spell, the fictive dream for us to pass out of her body and her time frame to jump ahead and read the future.

Write your story, then work backward and foreshadow later.

The great thing about foreshadowing is that you can do it at any stage of your writing process. So for you writers who hate to outline and just want to start writing and see where the characters and story take you, you can always go back through your manuscript later and plant clues and indications here and there to hint at major reversals and critical events. Doing this will not only increase the suspense and intrigue but will also improve the overall credibility and unity of your story.

So decide on the events you want to foreshadow and then work backward, planting hints about each event in earlier chapters. A small event might require only one subtle indication in the preceding chapter or at the start of the chapter in which it occurs. A major event occurring near the end of the novel can be hinted at and alluded to several times in the course of the novel.

And remember to sprinkle in the foreshadowing like a strong spice – not too much and not too little. If you give too many hints, you'll erode your suspense. If you don't give enough, readers might feel a bit cheated or manipulated when something unexpected happens, especially if it's a huge twist or surprise.

And again, the operative word is subtle. Don't hit readers over the head with it. Not all your readers will pick up on these little hints, and that's okay. It makes the ones who do feel all the more clever.

Remember that to be effective, foreshadowing needs to be subtle, like a whisper, not a shout.

According to Jessica Morrell, "foreshadowing serves a powerful purpose: It makes the important moments in fiction more potent because of the anticipation that came before."

Resources:
Lynn Franklin, "Literary Theft: Taking Techniques From the Classics." *The Journalist's Craft: A Guide to Writing Better Stories*, ed. by Dennis Jackson and John Sweeney. Allworth, 2002
Jessica Morrell, *Between the Lines*

Chapter 15 – DELAY, TEASE, AND STRETCH OUT THE MOMENT

WITHHOLDING INFORMATION, DELAYS, INTERRUPTIONS

Withholding information

A great way to build suspense and create anticipation is by teasing the reader with fragments of critical information and then delaying the big reveal – the payoff. Think of a slow, tantalizing striptease, where one item of clothing comes off at a time, with lots of flirting and playful manipulation to build up anticipation. Use the technique of delayed gratification by revealing critical details bit by bit, layer by layer. Getting glimpses of information and having to wait for more revealing details creates intrigue, curiosity, worry, and suspense. This compels the reader to become emotionally engaged and invested in the story, so they have to keep turning the pages.

As Jessica Morrell says, "There is no surer way to kill suspense than to answer every question before the reader wonders about it. Don't explain everything or answer every question up front or set things up too thoroughly, because this destroys suspense."

So don't reveal everything right away. Spread out your character's backstory and drop clues and innuendos as you go along about their dysfunctional family or shameful secrets, to keep the readers wondering, What's really going on here? What's going to happen next? What happened to her in the past? What's that all about?

Secrets and subterfuge

Either we, the readers, know something the hero doesn't, or he's working certain things out in his head and has crucial info he's revealing to us little by little – the clever author's way of keeping us on our toes, anxious and questioning, eager to keep reading.

Distractions and interruptions

Within scenes, heighten anticipation by using distractions and interruptions to delay long-awaited news, expected events or outcomes, resolutions of problems or conflicts, feared confrontations, etc.

Prolonging outcomes to delay the payoff

Even when writing a tense, critical scene, you can use little techniques to stretch out the moment for maximum effect. But don't annoy the readers by inserting trivia or anything off-topic or that doesn't suit the mood of the scene.

GO INTO SLOW-MOTION AND EXPAND THE MOMENT

At critical moments, stretch out the tension and suspense.
Years ago, I read this line by Hallie Ephron in isolation somewhere: "Write slow scenes fast and fast scenes slow." At the time, I really didn't get what she meant, but later I understood. Skip past slow, boring scenes by summarizing them or even leaving them out. But at a tense, intriguing moment, when you've got the reader on the edge of her seat and biting her nails, prolong the suspense and agony by slowing things down and stretching out the scene. Milk the moment for all it's worth. Or add an interruption and delay the resolution to a later scene.

As James Scott Bell says, "The more intense the tension, the longer you can draw it out."

So exploit and highlight suspenseful moments by slowing down time, drawing out the tension, and delaying the final revelation.

To stretch out the tension, show the critical details of your hero's struggles.
In a tense, life-or-death scene, increase the reader's apprehension

and worry by showing every detail of your heroine's battle to survive, including her feelings – fear, panic, urgency, determination.

For significant, tension-filled scenes, readers want to be riveted by every little critical detail, so show your threatened, desperate character panicking, frantically searching for solutions, weighing one against the other, making a critical decision, and acting, then reacting. Show her inner feelings and emotional and physical reactions during this process.

Here are some before-and-examples, disguised, from my editing of thrillers:

Setup: Cheryl and her husband have been held captive on a ship, and he's been thrown overboard, with his hands and feet still tied. The Coast Guard has just arrived. This is a desperate situation for Cheryl and her husband, which is at first resolved way too quickly, missing a perfect opportunity for bringing their anguish to life and adding stress and tension and suspense.

Before:

> "Don't worry about me—get my husband!" Cheryl screamed at the captain of the Coast Guard. "They threw him in the water!"

> "Focus the light on the water aft of the stern," the captain ordered.

> The search light found him immediately. He was struggling but his face was still above the surface.

> "Go get him," the captain ordered.

After:

> "Don't worry about me—get my husband!" Cheryl screamed at the captain of the Coast Guard. "They threw him in the water and his hands and feet are tied!"

"Focus the light on the water aft of the stern," the captain ordered.

The light searched the water for precious moments, without seeing him. Cheryl's heart was in her throat. *Where is he?* At last they heard splashing and gasping, then a desperate cry.

"Over there!" Cheryl shouted, pointing. They swung the light toward the sound and finally found Kyle. He was struggling and sputtering, his face barely above the surface.

"Go get him," the captain ordered.

Setup: Two people are being held captive in a basement, their hands and feet tied to the chairs.

Before:

"Can you get your hands free? I'm having no luck untying these knots."

"Shhh. They might hear us."

They stopped talking and went back to trying to untie the ropes.

After five minutes, Jenny whispered, "I'm free."

That was just too easy. Jenny got herself untied in only five minutes, without a great deal of effort, so the scene is lacking in delicious tension and suspense.

After:

"Can you get your hands free? I'm having no luck untying these knots."

"Shhh. They might hear us."

They stopped talking and went back to trying to untie the ropes.

Knowing their captors could return at any moment, Jenny concentrated on the task with renewed effort. After what seemed like an eternity, with several fingernails broken, she managed to loosen the knot around her wrists. "Finally! My hands are free. Now I can work on the ties around my ankles."

How the experts do it:

Take a lesson from Robert Crais, one of my favorite authors. In *The Sentry*, he slows down time and shows every little detail, to emphasize the importance of stealth and not being heard.

Instead of saying, "He jumped over the fence and used the key to open the back door," he shows us our hero Joe Pike's every move, to heighten the tension:

> He stepped into the shadows near the gate, then lifted himself over and dropped silently into the courtyard. He paused to listen, then felt for the key.

> He used a full minute to ease the key into the lock, another minute to turn the knob, and two full minutes to open the door. The entry was dark, fielding only a dim glow that escaped from above. Pike strained to catch sounds from the house, but heard nothing. Only then did he close the door.

For really critical scenes, where your protagonist is fighting for his life or struggling to defeat a formidable adversary, stretch out the tension even more. Look for places in your story where you move too quickly from stimulus to response, from the action of the antagonist to the protagonist's reactions, and miss an opportunity to draw out the tension and add to your readers' emotional engagement. Slow down time and show us the inner workings of your hero's mind, as he or she first reacts inwardly to the threat and then works out possible ways to solve the problem or gain the upper hand, then makes a decision and acts.

For example, in *Worth Dying For*, Lee Child expands time and uses pages to describe Jack Reacher's assessment of and confrontation with an adversary in a parking lot, which only takes seconds of real time. One sentence alone goes on for more than a page! And when Reacher lands the punch, we see the damage it's causing in detail inside and outside the opponent's body:

> Two hundred and fifty pounds of moving mass, a huge fist, a huge impact, the zipper of the guy's coat driving backward into his breastbone, his breastbone driving backward into his chest cavity, the natural elasticity of his ribcage letting it yield whole inches, the resulting violent compression driving the air from his lungs, the hydrostatic shock driving blood back into his heart, his head snapping forward like a crash test dummy, his shoulders driving backward, his weight coming up off the ground, his head whipping backward again and hitting a plate-glass window behind him with a dull boom like a kettle drum, his arms and legs and torso all going down like a rag doll, his body falling, sprawling, the hard polycarbonate click and clatter of something black skittering away on the ground, Reacher tracking it all the way in the corner of his eye, not a wallet, not a phone, not knife, but a Glock 17 semiautomatic pistol,..."

Find a moment of anxiety, fear, or terror in your novel and show your character's inner feelings and reactions in minute detail, to extend out the tension and build up the suspense. Perhaps she's captured, and the assailants will return any minute. Show her searching around her for anything that could help her get away or fight back. Here's where you show every detail of her surroundings, as some of the items she spots could help her escape or defend herself. But which ones? And how? Can she combine them somehow? Show the desperate workings of her mind and she searches her environment for anything that could help her escape. Build up the tension.

But don't do this by stretching out of the tension too often or it would start to lose its effectiveness. And most scenes don't warrant this kind of detail. Pick the most critical, high-voltage scenes to use this technique.

Resources:
James Scott Bell, *Conflict & Suspense*
Jessica Page Morrell, *Between the Lines*
Jodie's critical reading and editing of fiction

Chapter 16 – TWISTS, SURPRISES, EPIPHANIES, & REVELATIONS

What's the difference between an epiphany and a revelation?

Both concern important new insights and both usually change the course of the story. In an epiphany, a character has a sudden understanding or "Ah-ha!" moment, caused by connecting two seemingly unrelated details. Their epiphany usually causes a dramatic change in their attitude or thinking, significantly affecting their decisions and future. Revelations, on the other hand, can refer to changes in circumstances or new information revealed somehow, and can involve anyone or anything in the novel. Both epiphanies and revelations cause the story to veer off in a new direction.

EPIPHANIES

An epiphany is when a character, usually the protagonist, has a light-bulb moment of realization, which often changes everything for them. Put one of these sudden intuitive moments of enlightenment in the middle of your story to shake things up. This moment of understanding greatly enhances your character's growth and story arc and can also be the turning point your plot hinges on.

As Jessica Morrell says, "Epiphanies deepen characters, provide the high notes in the plot, trigger events, and cause, worsen, or resolve conflict." For maximum dramatic effect and reader satisfaction, be sure your protagonist's epiphany is earned through her inner struggles and searching, not by a stroke of luck or information given to her by someone else.

Epiphanies are normally positioned at "plot points" in the story. This is where the direction of the story changes significantly and moves in a new direction. A moment of epiphany grabs the reader's attention in a satisfying way, bringing us closer to the character and more involved in the story, as we all become "enlightened" at the same time.

Some examples of epiphanies or "eureka moments" in movies:

In *Independence Day*, a scientist's father tells him to dress more warmly so he doesn't catch a cold, which gives him the idea to disrupt the aliens' force fields by uploading a virus into the mother ship's computers in a reference to *The War of the Worlds*.

In *Inside Man*, a chance comment a rookie cop makes to Denzel Washington's character allows him to figure out exactly how the hostage takers were able to stay ten steps ahead of the police.

In the original *Stargate* movie, after two weeks of poring over a cartouche, Daniel Jackson finally figures out that the symbols aren't hieroglyphs but star constellations when he sees a picture of Orion on a guard's newspaper and recognizes the shape as one of the symbols.

In *A Few Good Men*, Tom Cruise briefly halts a brainstorming session with the rest of the defense team to look for his lucky baseball bat, which Demi Moore has innocently placed in the closet. Staring into the closet prompts a eureka moment that reveals an important fact about the case – the murder victim's clothes were hanging in his closet, and if he had really been due to transfer to another post the next morning – as his commanding officer has claimed – his things would have been packed, and his closet empty.

In *Men in Black*, the main characters have been racking their brains trying to figure out where the "Galaxy" is. Their only hint is that they were told by a dying alien that it's "on Orion's Belt." When Agent J sees his dog barking at a cat on the street, he realizes the alien meant bell, not belt – the cat's name is Orion, and the "Galaxy" is a trinket the size of a marble that is on the cat's collar where a bell would be.

In *The Man Who Knew Too Much*, Ben McKenna follows the lead of spy Louis Bernard's dying words, "Ambrose Chappell," to search for the kidnappers of Ben's son. Ben visits a taxidermy shop owned by a man named Ambrose Chappell, only to learn that Mr. Chappell has no association with the criminals. As Ben's wife, Jo, waits anxiously for him to return to their hotel room, one of her friends, Val, asks her the name of the person Ben's searching for. Val mistakenly calls him "Church," so after Jo corrects him with the word, "Chappell," she pauses, then exclaims, "It's not a man, it's a place! It's Ambrose Chapel!" Jo's friends help her find the address of the chapel in the phone directory, then she leaves to search there.

REVELATIONS

A revelation is when something the protagonist and the readers really want to know is finally revealed, found, or discovered. It can be a physical object like a letter or key, or a piece of information, like the code to unlock a safe or a door, the license plate of a car, a telephone number, or an address. It can be a critical secret from the past revealed, the identity of the murderer, the location of a cave, hidden room, or hideout, or the discovery of any other crucial piece of information. This pivotal discovery gives the story and the readers a jolt of adrenaline, as we want to find out what will happen now as a result of this new, critical information.

Figure out some objects or secrets that will be crucial to the unraveling of your plot, and withhold that information as long as you can, while hinting at them from time to time by showing your characters seeking those answers. Be sure to build up to the revelation to make the readers really want that information and continue reading eagerly to discover the secret or other critical knowledge or facts. This builds suspense and tension.

TWISTS, REVERSALS, REVELATIONS, AND SURPRISES

At every turn of events, at every character decision, think of the outcome or decision that readers are expecting, then brainstorm for unexpected alternate outcomes. To keep readers off-balance and maintain tension and suspense, try to often choose a result or decision that's unexpected.

The unexpected unsettles readers and makes them anxious, and anxiety and curiosity keep them turning the pages.

Lead the readers in one direction, then suddenly veer off course. The hero suffers an unexpected defeat or setback, which leads to a new dramatic outcome. But twists don't usually work if the is positive. A twist is like throwing a wrench in the works – it should add complications and increase the tension.

Try to put a big twist in the middle of your story and another big one at the end – the bigger, the better.

For examples of some excellent twists and revelations that left audiences reeling, have another look at some of these great movies:

In that old classic movie, *Citizen Kane* (1941), "Rosebud" turns out to be...

In the classic, ultra-creepy thriller, *Psycho* (1960), it turns out the old woman is actually....

In *The Planet of the Apes* (1968), the planet turns out to be...

In *Star Wars, Episode V: The Empire Strikes Back*, we're blown away by this revelation: "Luke, I am your ...."

In *The Usual Suspects*, a 1995 neo-noir film written by Christopher McQuarrie, the meek, mild, crippled Kevin Spacey character, "Verbal" Kint, turns out to actually be....

Similarly, in *Shutter Island*, written by Dennis Lehane, US Marshal

Teddy Daniels turns out to be...

In *Gone, Baby, Gone*, by Dennis Lehane, Amanda is actually...

In *The Prestige*, written by Christopher Priest, it turns out Borden has a...

In *Mystic River*, by Dennis Lehane, the killer isn't Dave Boyle, but rather...

Other famous surprise, ingenious twists at the ends of movies include the final revelations in *The Cabin in the Woods, The Sting, The Departed, American Psycho, Arlington Road, Memento, Fight Club*, and the most mind-boggling and memorable final twist of all, the ending of *Sixth Sense*, which left readers walking out of the movie with mouths hanging open, shaking their heads.

Don't get too crazy, though. Your twists should be surprising, even shocking, but in retrospect, they need to be justifiable and believable, given the preceding events, foreshadowing, etc. Readers need to be able to say, "Yes, that could happen."

Resources:
James Scott Bell, *Conflict & Suspense*
Lynn Franklin, "Literary Theft: Taking Techniques from the Classics," *The Journalist's Craft: A Guide to Writing Better Stories*, ed. by Dennis Jackson and John Sweeney
Jessica Page Morrell, *Between the Lines*
Jessica Page Morrell, *Thanks, But This Isn't For Us*

Chapter 17 – STORY CLIMAX, RESOLUTION, AND ENDING

Knock 'em dead with a kick-ass climax

Near the end of your book, you'll need to stage the major crisis, battle or confrontation of your novel, the one you've been building up to all along. This is the story climax, where typically, the hero is stretched to the limit. At his darkest moment, he almost loses, almost dies, but manages at the last possible moment to save himself and others and defeat evil. He does this by reaching deep inside himself and drawing out every last ounce of strength, courage, and resourcefulness he never knew he had.

This story climax is the pivotal scene with the highest stakes and most challenging difficulty of your whole novel. It's the scene you've been leading up to from the start. Finally, the hero manages to overcome the toughest obstacle, and the main story problem is resolved one way or another. Be sure that this critical no-holds-barred scene is the pinnacle of nail-biting conflict and suspense of your novel. If the greatest tension occurs earlier, then the ending of the story will feel anticlimactic and the readers will feel disappointed.

And try to include a twist at the end, too, to surprise and delight your readers. Conjure up something they didn't see coming but that can be justified by the details of the story, a turn of events that in retrospect seems plausible and makes sense, even though it didn't occur to them before.

Your readers have been living vicariously through your heroine, following her and worrying about her, right up through the final big climactic confrontation or battle, where she almost lost everything but managed to triumph over evil and adversity at the last possible moment. Now give them the payoff they're hoping for.

You are having her triumph, aren't you? Readers want to experience that huge sigh of relief when evil is defeated and justice prevails – at least for a while.

Create a memorable, satisfying ending

Now that you've written an engaging tale full of twists and turns, with lots of tension, conflict, suspense and intrigue, be sure to ice the cake with an ending that will leave readers satisfied and give them a sense of closure – and will make them want to read another story by you.

Don't forget that readers read fiction to identify with the characters and live their exciting adventures vicariously, suffering their ordeals with them, worrying about them, dreading that they'll fail, hoping and praying they'll succeed. As a reward for the time and emotions they've invested, readers want the emotional satisfaction of having the characters' problems resolved. They expect and want that huge feeling of relief when all the dramatic tension and suspense built up through the story is finally released.

So don't try to be clever or artsy and write in a tragic ending for your hero or heroine – unless you want readers to throw the book across the room in disgust.

That's not to say that every little bump in the road has to be smoothed out, but do resolve the main conflict and story dilemma positively for the protagonist. To be realistic, go ahead and show smaller defeats or losses along the way or near the end.

So my advice is to show how the hero barely manages to achieve his goal in the climax, then release all the reader's built-up tension with a satisfying, positive resolution of the hero's biggest problems. Save any innocent people who were threatened – or at least the ones closest to the hero, the people he cares about the most.

Or, if your hero doesn't achieve his main goal, maybe it turns out that wasn't the best goal for him, and the one he does achieve is a much higher goal, resulting in greater satisfaction and showing the growth he's gone through in the course of the story. He still goes through a positive character arc, which leaves him happier, wiser and more confident at the end.

You don't need to resolve every little story question – go ahead and leave a few hanging if you like. But for maximum reader satisfaction, tie up the major loose threads of the story. And a little romance in there wouldn't hurt!

Think back to all the movie and story endings you loved the most. They probably had a surprise "omigod!" twist near the end for an added jolt, followed by a quick "whew!" sense of relief, then an "ahhhh" moment of satisfaction.

Finally, try to leave the reader with some resonance, some intangible feeling of connecting to greater issues, to universal values. Something lasting to think about after they've closed the book.

PART VII

REVISE
FOR SUCCESS

Chapter 18 – REVISING FOR POWER

STYLE AND PACING FOR TENSION AND INTRIGUE

When you're revising your story, there are lots of little tricks to enhance the suspenseful moments for maximum reader engagement and enjoyment. Consider using these techniques at moments of high tension, when your character is racing or fighting for her life.

At stressful times:

Don't wax eloquent.
Minimize explanations, descriptions, thought processes, internal dialogue.

Declutter and write tight.
Use shorter, to-the-point sentences. Don't clutter up your sentences with blah, unneeded words or repetitions. Make every word count.

Before:
> Stan's mouth was dry and his eyes felt like they were full of sand. There was a nagging pain shooting from his eyes to the back of his head. A strong light hanging from the ceiling was shining in his face, and it must have been what had finally brought him around.

After:
> Dry mouth. Gritty eyes. Nagging pain shooting from his eye sockets to the back of his head. An industrial lamp above blinded him.

Show character reactions.

Bring the character and situation to life by showing us their thoughts, feelings, inner reactions, and physical sensations. Here's an example, well-disguised from my editing.

Setup: A man suspects his wife is cheating on him and discovers she's not only having an affair, but she's also plotting to have him killed.

Before:

> Craig opened Janine's purse that evening before they went out. He told himself he needed a pen. He found a note from a guy named Roy reminding her of their ren-dezvous tomorrow at a motel on the outskirts of town.
>
> The following day he came home and found her phone untended. He scanned through it and lost whatever hope he'd held. It was all so very much worse.

Jodie's comment: Maybe a mention of how he felt when he read the note, like shocked, bewildered, hurt. Or disbelief, followed by bewilderment, then anger...?

Then add more detail to the incident the next day, when he finds her phone. Build up the moment more for enhanced intrigue and tension.

After:

> Craig paced around the kitchen. Janine was acting strangely, avoiding him. What the hell is going on? He saw her purse on the table and decided to have a look through it while she was getting ready upstairs. Maybe he'd find some answers. He rifled through it quickly and pulled out her wallet. Inside with the bills was a folded piece of paper.
>
> Suppressing a moment of guilt at snooping, he opened it. It was a note from a guy named Roy reminding her of their rendezvous tomorrow at a motel on the outskirts of

town. The asshole even made some suggestions of what he was going to do to her and how she was going to love it.

Disbelief turned to bewilderment, then anger. What had he done to deserve this? Unable to deal with it all, he decided to try to find out more before confronting her.

The following day, when he got home from work, he heard the shower running. He quickly headed for their bedroom and checked through her purse again. He found her cell phone and opened it, scanning the text messages. He found one from Roy. As he read it, he lost whatever hope he'd held.

Not only was she cheating on him, but it was all so very much worse.

Show all critical action scenes in real time.

Never have one character tell another about a critical scene after the fact – back up and show it as it was happening earlier, with action, reactions, and dialogue, or go into a flashback that shows the scene unfolding in real time.

But summarize less important scenes in a sentence or two, if at all. And skip over transition periods, where characters going from one location to another, etc., unless you use that time for them to regroup and plan their next move. You can show the transition by an introductory phrase at the beginning of the next scene, like "Later that day," or "The next morning."

Leave out all irrelevant, distracting descriptive details.

Many newbie authors who haven't had the opportunity to work with a good editor will often clutter up fast-paced, run-for-your life scenes with nonessential description and meandering, convoluted sentences, which can really bog things down and deflate most of the tension. It's best to use short, tight sentences at tense moments and make every word count. And be sure to show your character's feelings and reactions, especially their tension and sense of urgency.

When your life or that of a loved one is on the line, there's no time or inclination for idle sightseeing. Notice how all the nonessential detail and almost carefree admiring of the idyllic surroundings slows down the pace and deflates the tension in the example below. The scene is in Boston.

> Jonathan raced up Arlington Street, hoping to make it to Boston Commons before they caught up with him. Maybe he could get lost in the Sunday crowd of families out enjoying the gorgeous spring day. Glancing back, he saw the men were gaining on him. Fortunately he was in much better shape, and not hampered as they were by suits and dress shoes.
>
> He ran the light on Boyleston and darted through an opening in the beautiful wrought-iron fence surrounding the park. The cherry trees with their profuse pink blossoms were stunning. As he ran down the path to the pond, he glanced to his left at the colorful tulips near the statue of George Washington on his horse. Ahead of him, the swan boats were out on the pond, and families with small children were strolling along the pathways.
>
> Jonathan ran to a crowd of Japanese tourists and started strolling along with them, on the far side. Keeping up with the tourists, he peered around them to see the goons hurrying toward him....

It would have been more effective to place Jonathan in an entirely different, more ominous or dangerous setting, and only highlight details that help or hinder his plight, focusing on his stress and attempts to get away, rather than positive aspects of his environment that aren't critical to his survival.

Pay attention to word choices and phrasing.

At times of regret, fear, danger, or stress, avoid using words with pleasant or relaxed connotations. Choose words that increase the tension rather than deflating it. Here's another well-disguised example from my editing:

Setup: This bad guy is being hunted and he knows it – it's payback time for all the horrible things he's done.

Before:

He buttoned his grey coat tightly, adjusted his hat snug on his head and walked out of the subway station and into the cold, to saunter back to his small apartment. It was yet another day whiling away his time around New York with no specific purpose other than contemplate the insecure future ahead of him.

Jodie's comments: The word "snug" conjures up feelings of comfort, which doesn't fit the tone you're going for here. And "saunter" seems too relaxed – both for the cold and his situation. Not to mention that tension is what drives fiction. Don't let your characters relax! Maybe have him hurry? Or "trudge"? And I'd have him worrying about his bleak future instead of whiling away his time. Also, replace "contemplate" with a word that shows his worry better.

After:

He buttoned his grey coat tight, pulled up his collar, adjusted his hat, and emerged from the subway station into the cold. He hurried along, head down, fighting the wind, back to his tiny apartment. Yet another day in New York with nothing but his bleak future weighing heavily on his mind.

Notice how the heavy mood is captured better with the revised, more ominous, negative imagery and wording.

At the revision stage, go back and use some or all of the above techniques to add apprehension, conflict and suspense to your story.

Chapter 19 – STRUCTURAL TIPS FOR AMPING UP TENSION AND INTRIGUE

Take a step back and look at the design and arrangement of your scenes and chapters to see if they maximize suspense and tension.

Vary the length of your chapters and scenes.
In general, thrillers suit shorter chapters, so forget the warm-up and cool-down and start each chapter late and end it early, with lots of cliffhangers and jump cuts. High-tension scenes and chapters should be even shorter, to mirror the urgency and leave the reader on edge.

Use cliffhangers.
For fast pacing and more tension and intrigue, end most scenes and chapters with some kind of surprising twist, intriguing story question, challenge, setback or threat. Ending a chapter with a startling revelation or leaving a conflict hanging and delaying its resolution piques the reader's curiosity and keeps her turning the pages.

How the experts do it:

Here's the ending of Chapter 2 of the riveting thriller *The Blade*, by Joe Moore and Lynn Sholes, which I had the pleasure of editing in 2012:

Setup: The protagonist, Maxine Decker, is hiding in the basement from an unknown home invader. She hears his big boots clomping on the floor, then he opens the basement door:

The second step creaked and then the third, slow and easy. A dark leather hiking boot settled on the step level with my face. The next step down, I grabbed his boot laces and he flew forward, head first. With a grunt, he hit the dirt floor hard. I ran out from under the stairs and before he could move, I had my knee planted firmly in his back at the base of his neck and the butt end of my Maglite pressed into his skull.

"Move and you're dead." I stabbed the Maglite against his head for emphasis, hoping it felt like the real thing.

"Maxine, sweetheart, is that any way to greet your long-lost love?"

And here's an intriguing chapter ending that raises a lot of questions in Dennis Lehane's heart-pounding thriller *Shutter Island*:

"What?" Teddy said.
Cawley shrugged. "I'm just confused."

"Confused by what?"

"You, Marshal. Is this some weird joke of yours?"

"What joke?" Teddy said. "I just want to know if he's here."

"Who?" Cawley said, a hint of exasperation in his voice.

"Chuck."

"Chuck?" Cawley said slowly.

"My partner," Teddy said. "Chuck."

Cawley came off the wall, the cigarette dangling from his fingers. "You don't have a partner, Marshal. You came here alone."

And I just had to share this great surprise twist at the end of a chapter in *Don't Look Twice*, by Andrew Gross:

Setup: The hero of the story, Ty Hauck, who's been threatened repeatedly, is being followed one night by a guy in a dark parka with a cap pulled over his face. Hauck creeps behind a row of cars to get the jump on his pursuer.

> Hauck wrapped a hand around his neck and jerked him backward, at the same time kicked out the guy's legs. The guy rolled onto the pavement with a grunt. Hauck dug a knee sharply into his back.
>
> "You wanted me, you got me, mister!" Hauck wrestled the man's arms behind him.
> The guy let out a groan.
>
> Hauck eased off his knee and spun him around. He pressed the barrel of his Sig into the man's face and a cell phone the guy had been carrying fell out of his hand.
>
> "Now what do you want, asshole?"
>
> He was staring into the face of his brother.

Employ scene cuts or jump cuts.
Create a series of short, unresolved incidents that occur in rapid succession. Stop at a tantalizing moment and jump to a different scene, often at a different time and place, with different characters – perhaps picking up from a scene you cut short earlier. Jump-cutting is a more extreme version of skipping ahead. This is used a lot in movies. You jump straight from one scene to another, with no transitioning at all in between.

Switch chapters or scenes quickly back and forth between your protagonist and antagonist(s), or from one dicey, uncertain situation to another. Don't resolve the conflict/problem before you switch to the next one.

Lynn Sholes and Joe Moore call this "bait and switch" and use it very skillfully to keep us breathlessly turning the pages. In their recent thriller *The Blade*, they jump back and forth for a while from the present in the U.S. to eighteen months earlier in Austria, with riveting scenes back to back on both continents. Then we're whisked off to nail-biting scenes in Cuba, including a shocking twist I never saw coming. Then the story takes us to more edge-of-your seat jump-cut scenes centered around Las Vegas. The technique is extremely effective in making the story difficult to put down.

Robert Dugoni also uses the jump-cut technique masterfully in his legal thriller *Murder One*, where he abruptly stops chapters and scenes at critical moments and leaves us hanging while he jumps to a new nail-biting scene, with no transition. Here's a scene ending from this novel:

> Sloan turned. "Look, just get your—"
>
> The man held open his leather car coat, displaying the butt of a handgun. A second man, also wearing a car coat, despite the heat and humidity, got out of a nearby parked car.
>
> And everything registered.
>
> Vasiliev.

And a chapter ending, later in Dugoni's novel:

> ...Rowe knocked on a door to their right, presumably the bedroom, and called out Oberman's name. When he got no answer, he pushed it open, ran his hand along the wall, and flipped another light switch.
>
> Stepping in, he said, "What the Sam Hill?"

Then the next chapter starts with different characters in another location. This unpredictable approach keeps readers off-balance, alert, and eager to find out what happens next.

Chapter 20 – RIVET YOUR READERS WITH SAVVY SENTENCE STRUCTURE AND SPACING

Think about how you can use the white space on your page as well as sentence and paragraph structure to help focus the readers, add tension and create the mood you're after.

Tricks for keeping your readers' interest and attention

Vary the length of your sentences.

All short sentences can seem choppy and staccato. All long sentences lack tension. Combining the two artfully adds variety and keeps readers on their toes.

A short example from *Something Wicked*, by Lisa Jackson and Nancy Bush:

> Lang slowly pulled the plastic bag nearer to get a closer look at the knife inside. "Catherine isn't the type to let out her secrets. Ever. What the hell is she doing?"

USE SENTENCE STRUCTURE TO ADD EMPHASIS

Power positions

If you put significant words at the end of the sentence, that's the last thought the reader is left with in that sentence, so that concept/idea stands out more and resonates with the reader.

Alternately, if you put a character's immediate inner reaction at the beginning of a paragraph, it stands out more and is more effective.

> *What!* She couldn't believe it.
> *Damn!* Where is that key?

Writing from a position of power

These are some of the power positions of words, courtesy of Elizabeth Lyon:
+ First and last words in a sentence
+ First and last sentences in a paragraph
+ First and last paragraphs in a chapter
+ First and last pages of a novel
+ First and last chapters of a novel

As Lyon says, "When a word, phrase, or sentence is in a first position, it serves as a hook to draw the reader in. The impact of the last position should cinch the meaning of the sentence or paragraph, and create suspense and curiosity leading to the next hook."

Notice the heightened impact of the placement of the first sentence and last word in this paragraph from Allison Brennan's *Love Me to Death*:

> Liquid date-rape drugs. Lucy dry heaved, waves of first fiery heat then icy cold coursing through her nerve endings. Her skin turned clammy, and she stumbled as she stood and ran to the bathroom, fearing she'd get sick.

Divide up long sentences to isolate each important point.
To create a pause for effect, give each important point its own sentence.

Don't run a bunch of important ideas in together in one long sentence, as each will be diminished a bit. Shorter sentences give a pause so the reader focuses more on the impact of each individual point made, each in its own sentence (or sentence fragment).

Here's an example from Sandra Brown's romantic suspense, *Chill Factor*:

> What a clever modus operandi. He befriended his victims. Romanced them into a sentimental stupor. Made sweet love to them. But at some point, the tender lovemaking turned violent.

Here's a great paragraph from Iris Johansen's *Stalemate*:

> All right, play it over so it couldn't sneak up on her. She closed her eyes. Black mamba striking at her. The drop cloth falling from her hand. The lamp hurling through the air. The snake coming. Coming. Coming. Montalvo shooting the snake. The snake was dead. Nothing to fear. Nothing to fear.

And one from Lisa Gardner's *The Neighbor*:

> ...if something doesn't give soon, I'm gonna plant my fist into his face. Or maybe not his face. Maybe the wall. Except maybe not the wall. Maybe the glass window. That will shatter my hand, and...

Add white space for emphasis.
Isolate critical points, words, or thoughts on their own line/paragraph, to underline their significance.

Tess Gerritsen shows us how, in her thriller, *Never Say Die*:

> ...He knew he couldn't stand the thought of her being hurt, that he'd do anything to keep her safe. Was love the name for that feeling?
>
> Somewhere in the night, an animal screamed.

He tightened his grip on the rifle.

Four more hours until dawn.

At first light the attack came.

Here's another example from Allison Brennan's *Love Me to Death*:

Setup: Lucy Kincaid, the protagonist, sees a headline in the news-paper and stops to read the story.

> She brought the paper to the kitchen table. Normally she didn't care about drug-related crimes, but since a student from a nearby college was involved, it piqued her interest.
>
> The story was shocking.

Having that last statement on its own line sets it apart and under-lines her feelings about the story. It definitely made me want to read on, to find out about the shocking story.

And here's Jack Reacher, in Lee Child's *Gone Tomorrow*, on his way to the hotel room of a woman named Lila:

> ...The lobby was quiet. I walked in like I had a right to be there and rode the elevator to Lila Hoth's floor. Walked the silent corridor and paused outside her suite.
>
> Her door was open an inch.
>
> The tongue of the security deadbolt was out and the spring closer had trapped it against the jamb. I paused another second and knocked.
>
> No response.
>
> I pushed the door and felt the mechanism push back. I held it open forty-five degrees against my spread fingers and listened.

No sound inside.

And it goes on like this.

For even more emphasis, start a new line for the important sentence, sentence fragment, or word, then end the scene or chapter. So a bit of white space, the word or sentence, then the scene or chapter ends, so the significant word or sentence resonates into space.

Here's an example from Dennis Lehane's *Shutter Island* of ending a chapter with an intriguing last line – the thoughts of the protagonist, Teddy:

How the hell did I get shoe polish on my thumbs?

Use sentence fragments.
Use partial sentences or sentence fragments often in dialogue and thoughts, and at other times to pick up the pace and add to a feeling of rushing, breathlessness, fright, impatience, anger, confusion or annoyance.

Or, conversely, sentence fragments with frequent periods can create a feeling of stopping briefly to focus on each detail, one after the other, rather than skipping along.

Here's an example from a Jack Reacher thriller, *The Hard Way*, by Lee Child:

... Reacher followed him to the master bedroom suite. The pencil post bed, the armoire, the desk. The silence. The photograph. Lane opened his closet. The narrower of the two doors. Inside was a shallow recess, and then another door. To the left of the inner door was a security keypad. It was the same type of three-by-three-plus zero matrix as Lauren Pauling had used at her office. Lane used his left hand. Index finger, curled. Ring finger, straight. Middle finger, straight. Middle finger, curled. 3785, Reacher thought. Dumb or distracted to let me see. The keypad beeped and Lane opened the inner door. Reached inside to pull a chain....

Notice how effective the short staccato sentences and sentence fragments are to illustrate Reacher's concentration and attention to every little visual in the room and the critical details of opening of the safe.

At other times, Lee Child will use great long run-on sentences for other effects, like racing or breathlessness.

For emphasis, use the occasional one- or two-word sentence.

According to Elizabeth Lyon, "One-word sentences are a stop sign. They make the reader slam on the brakes with sudden awareness of stopping. The sleepwalking reader wakes up. One-word sentences have power." But be sure you don't waste that power by squandering it on a meaningless or ordinary word, one unworthy of the emphasis.

Here's an example of a strong word singled out for more emphasis.

> What a tragedy. Senseless. She sat, shoulders slumped, fighting back the tears.

The Hunger Games:

Katniss has been badly stung by nasty tracker jacker wasps.

> The swelling. The pain. The ooze. Watching Glimmer twitching to death on the ground.

Use rapid-fire dialogue.

At times of high conflict, tension, or stress, for dialogue, use short, terse sentences, sentence fragments, interruptions, evasions, and silences. Short, even one-word or two-word questions and answers pick up the pace and add punch and tension.

Here's an excellent example from David Morrell's riveting thriller *The Brotherhood of the Rose:*

Setup: Saul, the protagonist, exhausted, cold, and wounded, is trying to talk a truck driver into giving him a ride.

The driver stiffened when he saw him.

"Fifty bucks for a ride," Saul said.

"Against the rules. You see that sign? No passengers. I'd lose my job."

"A hundred."

"So you mug me when you get the chance. Or your buddies hijack the truck."

"Two hundred."

The driver pointed. "Blood on your clothes. You've been in a fight, or you're wanted by the cops."

"I cut myself shaving. Three."

"No way. I've got a wife and kids."

"Four. That's my limit."

"Not enough."

"I'll wait for another driver." Saul walked toward a different truck.

"Hey, buddy."

Saul turned.

"That kind of money, you must really need to get out of town."

"My father's sick."

The driver laughed. "And so's my bank account. I hoped you'd offer five."

"Don't have it."

"Ever seen Atlanta?"

"No," Saul lied.

"You're going to." The driver held out his hand. "The money."

"Half now."

And so on. I could easily keep reading and typing! This is also an excellent example of natural-sounding dialogue between two tough males.

Resources:
Elizabeth Lyon, *Manuscript Makeover*
Jodie's reading and editing of thrillers

Chapter 21 – TIGHTEN YOUR WRITING AND PICK UP THE PACE

In a suspense-thriller (or any compelling fiction), it's important to write succinctly and economically. There's no place for long descriptions or lengthy philosophizing or meandering sentences. Leave that to more leisurely genres. Your paragraphs and sentences need to be tight, and your language needs to be concrete, vivid, sensory, concise, and to the point. Almost every sentence should have some tension or movement in it, and every paragraph should advance the plot or contribute to characterization.

As Steve Berry says: "Shorter is always better. Write tight. It makes you use the best words in the right way." Succinct, to-the-point writing produces the fast pace demanded by thrillers.

Don't meander or ramble. Don't wax eloquent. Don't use obtuse, show-offy words that will send your readers to the dictionary. Direct, evocative words are much more powerful. Avoid the convoluted, erudite sentence structure popular in previous centuries. And don't say the same thing three or four times in different ways – we got it the first time! Also, stay away from stale clichés.

As Harlan Coben says about writing his thrillers, "I want it to be compulsive reading. So on every page, every paragraph, every sentence, every word, I ask myself, 'Is this compelling? Is this gripping? Is this moving the story forward?' And if it's not, I have to find a way to change it.... No word really should be wasted."

TIPS FOR WRITING TIGHTER

In general, declutter paragraphs and sentences.
Get your scissors and see where you can snip. Try to take one un-needed or weak word (or more) out of most sentences, and one super-fluous sentence or more out of medium and long paragraphs. Can some entire paragraphs be deleted? Or most of their contents? Make every word count. And of course tighten any scenes that start too early or go on for too long. And delete any scenes that aren't pulling their weight.

Here are some before-and-after examples, disguised, from vari-ous novels I've edited, to demonstrate how cutting out superfluous words to streamline paragraphs and sentences results in greater impact:

Setup: A tense, edgy scene in a bar. As originally written, it's too wordy and conversational, almost meandering, when terse would be more effective to mirror the tension of the situation:

Before:
> Then he continued, speaking just loudly enough to be heard by Chad but not by any of the surrounding drink-ers, not that anyone seemed to be listening. "Here's what we're going to do," he said.

After:
> Then he continued in a low voice, "Here's what we're going to do."

And from a different novel:

Before:
> "Let's check the nearby neighbors ourselves," Steve said, and looked around. "Mostly young families, so they should have been home last night," Steve suggested. If she was killed somewhere besides in her own home, he had to find that place, and finding her car might tell him something about where she had been before she was killed.

After:

> "Let's check the nearby neighbors ourselves." Steve looked around. "Mostly young families, so they should have been home last night." If she was killed somewhere else, finding her car might give them some clues as to where.

And from yet another novel:

Before:

> And on the side, he moonlighted as a consultant for an electrical engineering company just to make some extra bucks.

Jodie's comment: "on the side", "moonlighted" and "just to make some extra bucks" all mean basically the same thing.

After:

> He also moonlighted as a consultant for an electrical engineering company.

Or how about this one:

Before:

> George just smiled and let it go. He was discreet like that. He wouldn't try to force more information out of Perry, because he was the kind of friend who was happy to help without the need to ask too many questions to satisfy his own curiosity.

After:

> George just smiled and let it go. He was discreet like that—the kind of friend who was happy to help without asking a lot of questions.

Still another:

Before:

> He wore a plain red baseball cap with, a white cotton shirt, and a pair of jeans that had faded from their original color

to a nondescript shade of something.

Jodie: There are a lot of extra words after "jeans" that don't really add much of anything, just clutter up the sentence.

After:
He wore a plain red baseball cap, a white cotton shirt, and faded jeans.

And finally...

Before:
He could hardly believe it was real. He wanted this to be a bad dream he would wake up from. His racing heart overpowered his lungs and it didn't seem like they were taking in any air with any measure of efficiency.

After:
This can't be happening. It has to be a bad dream. His racing heart overpowered his lungs, which couldn't seem to take in air.

Now go through your whole manuscript and....

Take out empty phrases.
Jump right in and say what you're talking about. Not "There was a cat lying on the windowsill," but "A cat was lying on the windowsill."

Take out qualifiers.
Don't be wishy-washy – be bold! Instead of saying "The sight of the wound made her feel kind of sick," say "The sight of the wound made her sick."

Delete almost every instance of "very."
"She was beautiful" is more powerful than "She was very beautiful."

Take out almost all synonyms for "said" or "asked."
Just use said or asked most of the time, except for instances like shouted, yelled, screamed, or whispered, which are useful.

Delete most -ly adverbs.

"He walked loudly across the floor" or "he said angrily," or "she asked timidly" are flabby. Let a character's words and actions show how they're feeling or talking and use a stronger verb that gives the same impression all by itself, like "he stomped across the floor," or "he shouted," or "she pleaded."

Fix repetitions of words or words in the same family.

In the same paragraph or on the same page, words like respect, respected, respectfully, disrespectful; help, helping, helpful, helpless, etc., lacks originality.

Replace bland, overused verbs.

Walked, ran, looked, went, saw, ate, etc., should yield to more vivid ones.

Replace passive constructions with active ones.

"The knife was thrown by the man" vs. "the man threw the knife."

Cut most of those clichés.

Look for overused tired expressions and try to replace them with a fresh new way of saying the same thing.

Keep exclamation points and semicolons to a minimum.

For a lot more detail, with examples, of cutting the clutter and streamlining your writing to increase the power and impact of your words, see my book *Fire up Your Fiction – An Editor's Guide to Writing Compelling Stories*.

Let's finish off this chapter with some guidelines from an expert.

ELMORE LEONARD'S 10 RULES FOR WRITING FICTION

Excerpted from Leonard's article on writing, published July 16, 2001, in the *New York Times* and available in full online.

Leonard is the author of gritty westerns, crime novels and thrillers.

Among his best-known works are *Get Shorty, Out of Sight, Freaky Deaky, Hombre, Mr. Majestyk*, and *Rum Punch*, which was filmed as *Jackie Brown*. Leonard's short stories include ones that became the films *3:10 to Yuma* and *The Tall T*, as well as a current TV series on FX, *Justified*.

(I've condensed Leonard's explanations for the sake of brevity.)

WRITERS ON WRITING; Easy on the Adverbs, Exclamation Points and Especially Hooptedoodle

These are rules I've picked up along the way to help me remain invisible when I'm writing a book, to help me show rather than tell what's taking place in the story. If you have a facility for language and imagery and the sound of your voice pleases you, invisibility is not what you are after, and you can skip the rules. Still, you might look them over.

1. Never open a book with weather.
If it's only to create atmosphere, and not a character's reaction to the weather, you don't want to go on too long. The reader is apt to leaf ahead looking for people.

2. Avoid prologues.
They can be annoying, especially a prologue following an introduction that comes after a foreword. ... A prologue in a novel is backstory, and you can drop it in anywhere you want.

3. Never use a verb other than "said" to carry dialogue.
The line of dialogue belongs to the character; the verb is the writer sticking his nose in. But said is far less intrusive than grumbled, gasped, cautioned, lied.

4. Never use an adverb to modify the verb "said"...
...he admonished gravely. To use an adverb this way (or almost any way) is a mortal sin. The writer is now exposing himself in earnest, using a word that distracts and can interrupt the rhythm of the exchange.

5. Keep your exclamation points under control.

6. Never use the words "suddenly" or "all hell broke loose."
... I have noticed that writers who use "suddenly" tend to exercise less control in the application of exclamation points.

7. Use regional dialect, patois, sparingly.
Once you start spelling words in dialogue phonetically and loading the page with apostrophes, you won't be able to stop.

8. Avoid detailed descriptions of characters.

9. Don't go into great detail describing places and things.
...even if you're good at it, you don't want descriptions that bring the action, the flow of the story, to a standstill.

10. Try to leave out the parts that readers tend to skip.
Think of what you skip reading a novel: thick paragraphs of prose you can see have too many words in them. ... I'll bet you don't skip dialogue.

My most important rule is one that sums up the 10.

If it sounds like writing, I rewrite it.

Or, if proper usage gets in the way, it may have to go. I can't allow what we learned in English composition to disrupt the sound and rhythm of the narrative. It's my attempt to remain invisible, not distract the reader from the story with obvious writing. (Joseph Conrad said something about words getting in the way of what you want to say.)

If I write in scenes and always from the point of view of a particular character – the one whose view best brings the scene to life – I'm able to concentrate on the voices of the characters telling you who they are and how they feel about what they see and what's going on, and I'm nowhere in sight.

Resources:
Jodie's editing
New York Times article

PART VIII

WRAP-UP AND CHECKLISTS

Chapter 22 – Wrap-Up: ESSENTIAL ELEMENTS OF A BESTSELLING THRILLER

If you want your thriller or other suspense fiction to be a riveting page-turner, make sure you've included most or all of these elements:

A compelling opening
Don't rev your engines with a lengthy description of the setting or background on the character's life. Jump right in with your protagonist in a tension-filled scene with someone important in his world.

Deep POV
Start your story in the head of your main character, in close third-person viewpoint, or first-person. Deep point of view is the most intimate and compelling, and engages the reader fast.

A protagonist who's both ordinary and heroic
Rather than having a "Superman," invincible-type hero, it's usually more satisfying to the readers if you use a regular person who's thrown into stressful, then increasingly harrowing situations, who must summon all of his courage, strength and inner resources to overcome the odds, save himself and other innocent people, and defeat evil. Readers relate more personally to this type of main character and bond with him better.

A likeable, sympathetic protagonist
The readers need to be able to warm up to your main character quickly, to start identifying with her; otherwise they won't really

care what happens to her. So no cold, selfish, arrogant characters for heroes or heroines!

A worthy adversary for the protagonist

Your antagonist/villain needs to be as clever, strong, resourceful and determined as your protagonist, but also truly nasty, immoral, and frightening.

An interesting setting

Readers like to find out about places they haven't been, whether it's the seedy side of Chicago, glitzy Hollywood, rural Kentucky, the mountains of Colorado, or the bayous of Louisiana – or more distant, exotic locations. And milk your setting for all it's worth. Also, show the setting through the senses and reactions of your viewpoint character.

An inciting incident

What happens to the main character to set the story events in action? Make it tense and compelling, something he can't turn away from.

Internal struggling of the protagonist

Give her a moral dilemma; show his inner conflict. Make them complex and fascinating; never perfect, complacent, or overly confident.

A crucible

According to Steve Berry, the essential crucible is "that thing that gets a character to do what they normally will never do." It's a set of circumstances the protagonist can't escape from, so he has to go forward, through it. Also called the cauldron.

A riveting plot, with ongoing conflict and tension

You need a big story question and plenty of intrigue. And every scene should contain tension and conflict of some kind. If it doesn't, revise it or delete it.

Lots of suspense and intrigue

Keep the readers on the edge of their seats, turning the pages to find out what's going to happen next.

Multiple viewpoints

Narrating the story from various points of view, including that of the villain, will add interest, complexity and suspense to your novel. But most of the story should be in your protagonist's POV, and don't head-hop within a scene! Wait for a new scene or chapter to change viewpoints.

A tight, fast-paced writing style

Streamline your writing to improve flow and pacing. Go through and take out all unnecessary words, sentences, and paragraphs, and any repetitive phrases, events or ideas. Thrillers are not the genre to wax eloquent or show off your erudition. See my book *Fire up Your Fiction – An Editor's Guide to Writing Compelling Stories*.

Emotions and reactions

Engage the readers more and bring your characters to life on the page by showing their fear, trepidation, panic, pain, worry, anger, determination, courage, satisfaction, relief, joy, despair, elation, and other emotions.

Vivid sensory descriptions

Put the reader right there in the scene by using all five senses wherever possible. Show what the character is hearing, smelling, feeling, touching and tasting, not only what they're seeing.

Increasing danger

Keep raising the stakes and putting your hero in deeper and deeper trouble to stretch his courage, determination, physical abilities, and inner resources to the maximum – and increase the reader's admiration and emotional investment in him!

A ticking clock

Your hero is racing against time to defeat the villain before innocents are killed – or even the region, country, or whole world is imperiled. Adding ever-increasing time constraints increases the tension and suspense.

Troubles that hit home

Endanger the protagonist or someone close to her to add a personal dimension and more stress to the threats and conflicts.

Critical turning points
Present your hero with life-or-death decisions and show his anxiety, tension, and indecision.

Obstacles in the way
Your heroine runs out of gas on a lonely road; your hero's weapon falls into the river far below; he is wounded and can't run; her cell phone battery is dead. Whatever can go wrong does, and more.

Enough clues
Be fair. Use foreshadowing, and layer in clues and info as you go along to slowly reveal the plot points, character backstory, and motivation to the reader.

Twists and surprises
Write in a few unexpected plot twists, but make sure that, in retrospect, they make sense to the readers.

A compelling climax
Put the protagonist at a disadvantage in the final conflict with the antagonist to heighten the stakes. Pile on the adversity the hero has to overcome at the end.

A surprising but satisfying ending
Leave the unhappy or unresolved endings for literary fiction. Let the good guy overcome the bad guy – by a hair.

Psychological growth and change in the hero/heroine
Adversity has made him or her stronger, braver, wiser — a better person.

Chapter 23 – CHECKLIST FOR RATCHETING UP THE TENSION AND SUSPENSE

Finally, let's wrap up with a handy checklist.

It's a given that thrillers and other fast-paced popular fiction need lots of tension, suspense, and intrigue. But so does any other compelling story that'll create a buzz and take off in sales. No matter what genre you write, it's all about hooking your readers in, engaging them emotionally, and ensuring they keep eagerly turning the pages.

Here's a great list of essentials for ratcheting up the tension and suspense of your novel or short story. Use as many of these elements and devices as possible to increase the "wow" factor of your fiction.

Plan and set up a riveting story:

___ Give readers a sympathetic, charismatic, but flawed protagonist they'll identify with and start worrying about.

___ Create a nasty, cunning, believable villain (or other antagonist) to instill fear and anxiety.

___ Devise a significant, meaningful story problem, a serious dilemma for your hero, preferably a threat with far-reaching consequences.

___ Make it personal to your protagonist. She and/or her loved ones are personally threatened.

Bring your protagonist and story to life on the page:

___ Use close point of view (deep POV) and stay inside the head of your protagonist most of the time, for maximum reader engagement.

___ Show your main character's reactions to people and events around him.

___ Evoke all five senses – what is she seeing, hearing, smelling, touching, and tasting?

___ Show his inner fears, anxieties, anger, and frustrations.

___ Use occasional brief flashbacks in real time to reveal her secrets and fears, deepen characterization, and strengthen reader involvement.

___ Use alternating viewpoints – put us in the head of your protagonist and antagonist (or, in a romantic suspense, the female and male leads).Give them each their own scenes or chapters, so readers find out what the antagonist is thinking and planning, too. But stay mostly in your protagonist's POV to keep us bonded with her.

Pile on the problems:

___ Keep raising the stakes for your protagonist. Just as he solves one problem, he's confronted with a worse obstacle or dilemma.

___ Hamper your hero or heroine at every turn – the gun is jammed or falls into the river, the door is locked, the cell phone battery is dead, the car runs out of gas, there's a roadblock ahead ...

___ Isolate your lead character. She's all alone – her support system is gone.

___ Give her tough choices and moral dilemmas. The right decision is the most difficult one; the morally wrong choice is the easy way out.

Set the tone with style, mood, and pacing:

___ Use ominous setting details to add to the stress and anxiety.

___ Show, don't tell. Don't intrude as the author, and minimize explanations and backstory.

___ Write tight. Make every word count.

___ Vary your sentence structure to suit the situation and mood.

___ Use distinctive, vivid verbs and nouns rather than overused, generic ones like "walked" or "ran."

___ Use strong imagery and just the right word choices to set the mood.

___ Vary the pacing and tension. Nonstop action can be exhausting.

Pay attention to chapter and scene structure:

___ Don't spend a lot of time on lead-up or wind-down. Start chapters late and end them early.

___ Make sure every scene has some conflict and a change.

___ Use cliffhangers frequently at the end of chapters – but not always.

___ Employ some jump cuts – end a chapter suddenly, without resolving the issue, then start the next chapter with different characters in a different scene.

___ Show all critical scenes in real time, with tension, action, reactions, and dialogue.

___ Skip past or quickly summarize transitions and unimportant scenes.

Experiment with these devices to increase suspense and intrigue:

___ Sprinkle in some foreshadowing – drop subtle hints and innuendos about critical plot points or events.

___ Withhold information – use delay tactics, interruptions at critical points.

___ Stretch out critical scenes – milk them for all they're worth.

Surprise or shock your readers:

___ Add in a few unexpected twists. Put a big one in the middle and another big one at the end.

___ Use surprise revelations from time to time – reveal character secrets and critical information the reader has been dying to know.

___ Have your main character experience at least one epiphany – a sudden significant realization that changes everything for them. Try putting one in the middle and one near the end.

___ Write in reversals of feelings, attitudes, expectations, and outcomes.

Keep adding more tension. Increase the troubles of your protagonist by using these plot devices:

___ Ticking clocks – every second counts.

___ Obstacles, hindrances – keep challenging your hero or heroine.

___ Chases – your protagonist is chasing or being chased.

___ Threats or hints of more danger ahead.

___ Traps and restrictions – your character becomes somehow trapped and must use all their resources to get out of the situation.

Create a memorable, satisfying ending:

___ Design a big showdown scene, an extremely close battle between the hero/heroine and the villain.

___ Write in a surprise twist at the end.

___ Leave your readers satisfied – the hero wins by a hair, the main story question/conflict is resolved.

*****

Do you have a moment to leave a review? If you have found this book helpful in planning, writing, or revising your first or any subsequent thriller or other fast-paced fiction, I'd love it if you could leave a review on Amazon under the title of this book. Thanks a lot!

– Jodie Renner

PART IX

OTHER RELATED INFO

GLOSSARY OF FICTION TERMS

Average lengths of literary works:

These are rough guidelines, and there is often a bit of overlap. Individual publishers' word-count guidelines may vary.

Flash fiction: A story that is less than 500 words.

Short short story: A story roughly 500 to 1000 words.

Short story: A story that's usually between 1,000 and 7,500 words.

Novelette: A story roughly between 7500 and 17,500 words. (Some consider the term novelette to be outdated.)

Novella: Fiction that falls between a short story and a novel; usually between 17,500 and 50,000 words long.

Novel: Fiction that is about 50,000 or more words long.

Definitions of some of the many common terms used to describe fiction writing:

Antagonist: The main character or force in fiction that tries to stop the protagonist (the hero or heroine of the story) from achieving his/her goal.

Antihero: A protagonist who has no (or few) heroic virtues or

WRITING A KILLER THRILLER

qualities (such as being morally good, idealistic, courageous, noble), blurring the line between hero and villain. Often go through a character arc to become more heroic by the end of the story. An antihero is a protagonist who has the opposite of most of the traditional attributes of a hero. (S)he may be amoral, bitter, rebellious, bewildered, ineffectual, deluded, or even apathetic.

Archetypes: Certain character traits that appear in many stories, like the alpha male or the virginal heroine.

Backstory: The events of character's life up to the point of the first page of the story; the character's past.

Cauldron: When the hero is stuck in the thick of things. He can't escape or turn back so he must go forward and try to defeat the adversary.

Character arc: how a character (usually the protagonist) changes from the beginning to the end of a story as a result of the story events and their experiences throughout the story. In popular fiction, most protagonists go through a noticeable character arc by the end. (Not so much for the tough heroes in action-adventure novels.)

Characterization: The author's depiction of a character's personality through the use of action, dialogue, thought, or commentary.

Cliché: A trite, stereotyped expression; a sentence or phrase, usually expressing a popular or common thought or idea, that has lost originality, ingenuity, and impact by long overuse; a trite or hackneyed plot, character development, etc.; anything that has become trite or commonplace through overuse.

Cliffhanger: A suspenseful situation occurring at the end of a chapter, scene, or episode; an exciting, suspenseful end to a scene or chapter that makes readers want to continue reading.

Climax: The moment of greatest intensity in a story, usually the point where the central character/protagonist faces and deals with the consequences of all his/her actions.

Cozy mystery: A mystery where there is little or no violence; the emphasis is on solving the crime. The protagonist is often an amateur detective.

Crucible: See Cauldron. Heroine can't escape the situation or turn around and go home. She must continue to confront the villain and try to defeat him to restore justice.

Dénouement: The resolution of the story, where the main conflict is resolved and the main story question is answered. The protagonist is usually victorious and the villain is usually defeated.

Deus ex machina: A Latin term meaning "god out of the machine." It refers to an unexpected, artificial or improbable character, device or event introduced suddenly in a work of fiction to resolve a situation or untangle a plot. Considered a weakness and last-minute, lazy plotting.

Dramatic irony: This is when your readers know something vital the protagonist or other main character is not aware of.

Epiphany: A sudden, intuitive, significant realization or discovery; a revealing scene or moment, usually by the protagonist.

Flashback: A sudden, vivid reversion to a past event. It is used to surprise the reader with previously unknown information that provides the answer to a mystery, places a character in a different light, or reveals the reason for a previously inexplicable action.

Foreshadowing: The presentation of details, characters, or incidents in a narrative in such a way that later events are prepared for (or "shadowed before"). A hint of events that may and usually do follow later in the story (the poker lying by the fireplace in the first paragraph will turn out to be the murder weapon later in the story). Foreshadowing is often used to create suspense.

Genre: A type of literature. A novel, story, or other literary work belongs to a particular genre if it shares at least a few conventions, or standard characteristics, with other works in that genre. The main genres of fiction are mystery, romance, thriller, western, fantasy, historical, speculative, and horror.

Hard-boiled mystery: A mystery containing at least some violence and tough private eyes or cops.

High concept: A storyline that can easily be described in one sentence and seems to be especially unique and commercially viable.

Historical fiction: Any fiction set in the past.

Hook: A narrative trick in the opening paragraph of that grabs the attention of the readers and keeps them reading.

Horror story: A story, movie, etc., that entertains or fascinates by shocking or frightening, especially by an emphasis on bloodshed or supernatural forces.

In medias res: Beginning the story in the middle of the action.

Literary fiction: Fiction that is devoted to the literary aspects of writing, with the emphasis being on the style of writing rather than on the art of storytelling.

Mainstream fiction: Realistic stories of people, the tragedies and joys they may experience, and the decisions and choices they may face throughout life.

McGuffin: A common plot device used in films and novels, especially mysteries. Basically used to distract the reader from the real issues. It's an image or object or place that is referred to occasionally to spark interest, but which ultimately turns out not to be significant or relevant to the plot.

Mystery stories: Stories in which the main character is trying to solve a crime, usually a murder, and apprehend the criminal. Can have varying levels of violence and suspense, depending on the sub-genre.

Narrative: A collection of events that tells a story, which may be true or not, placed in a particular order.

Narrator: One who tells a story, the speaker or the "voice" of an oral or written work. The narrator is not usually the same person as the author. The narrator is most often the protagonist or other important participant, but can be an observer or even a non-participant.

Omniscient narrator: Non-participant, third-person, all-knowing narrator who sees into the minds of all the characters. Like the author talking to the readers about the characters and story. Rarely used in current popular fiction.

Plot: The story line or pattern of events in a story; the basic idea of the story, the action that moves the story from the beginning to the end.

Plot arc: story arc. The main events of your story, connected by cause and effect.

Plot device: a means of advancing the plot in a story, often used to motivate characters, create urgency, or resolve a difficulty. This can be contrasted with moving a story forward with narrative technique; that is, by making things happen because characters take action for well-motivated reasons. As an example, when the cavalry shows up at the last moment and saves the day, that can be argued to be a plot device; when an adversarial character who has been struggling with himself saves the day due to a change of heart, that is dramatic technique. (Wikipedia)

Plot hole: A gap or inconsistency in a storyline that goes against the flow of logic established by the story's plot, or constitutes a blatant omission of relevant information regarding the plot, sometimes even contradicting itself. A plot hole is a major gaffe or oversight that is essential to the story's outcome, and includes: unlikely behavior or actions of characters, illogical or impossible events, events happening for no apparent reason, or statements/events that contradict earlier events in the storyline.

Plot twist: A change in the expected direction or outcome of the plot of a novel, film, television series, etc. It's a device used to keep the interest of the readers or audience, usually surprising them with a revelation. Some "twists" are foreshadowed.

Point of view (abbreviation: POV): The viewpoint in which the story is told (first, second or third person; close point of view, omniscient, etc.). First-person POV: The story as told by one of the characters in the story: I ran across the street. Third-person POV: As seen through the eyes of one of the characters in the story: She ran across the street. Second-person POV (rarely used) is as seen through the eyes of the reader: You run across the street.

POV: Abbreviation for point of view or viewpoint

Premise: The question or problem that is the basic idea of a story.

Protagonist: The main character or hero of a story whose actions and goal drive the plot.

Red herring: A literary device that leads readers or characters toward a false conclusion, often used in mystery or detective fiction.

Revelation: Something that is revealed in the course of your story, something your characters or readers discover that was hidden, and which usually affects the plot by changing the course of decisions, actions and events.

Reversal: The situation at the end of a scene or chapter is the opposite of what it was at the beginning. Can apply to characterization or plot points.

Setting: The time, place, physical details, and circumstances in which a situation occurs. Settings include the background, atmosphere or environment in which characters live and move, and usually include physical characteristics of the surroundings.

Show versus tell: "Show" puts us there with the character in real time, with action and dialogue. Shows what characters experience through their five senses. "Tell" is the author's narration, or a character telling another character about an event after the fact.

Storyline: Plot or plotline – the main events of the story, told in order, with cause and effect.

Style: Individual traits and characteristics of a piece of writing; a writer's particular way of managing words, the language a writer uses, length and complexity of sentences, habitual use of imagery, patterns of sound, etc.

Subgenre: A category within a genre of fiction. Some subgenres of thrillers are psychological thrillers, legal thrillers, romantic suspense, medical thrillers, and historical thrillers.

Subplot: A secondary story within a novel, complete and interesting in its own right, that reinforces or contrasts with the main plot.

Subterfuge: In fiction, an evasive tactic or device used to conceal or hold back information for a while.

Theme: The central meaning or dominant idea in a literary work. It is the unifying point around which the plot, characters, setting, point of view, symbols, and other elements of a work are organized.

Thriller: A broad genre of literature, film, and television programming that uses suspense, tension, and excitement as the main elements. Thrillers heavily stimulate the reader's or viewer's moods, giving them a high level of anticipation, ultra-heightened expectation, uncertainty, surprise, anxiety, and/or terror. Thriller films tend to be adrenaline-rushing, gritty, rousing, and fast-paced. (Wikipedia)

Thrusters: "Thrusters are structural devices that push the story ahead, move the action forward, and raise questions or cause curiosity about unanswered issues or things to come." (Jessica Page Morrell)

Tone: The author's implicit attitude toward the reader or the people, places, and events in a work as revealed by the elements of the author's style; the author's choice of details, character, event, and situations, and words that lead us to infer an overall attitude for the book or a particular scene: amusement, anger, affection, sorrow, contempt, hate.

Tropes: Conventions and devices found within creative works; a common or overused theme or device: cliché "the usual horror movie tropes"; a figure of speech using words in nonliteral ways, such as a metaphor.

Twist: In fiction, a turn of events that is totally unexpected, used to surprise and/or shock readers.

Unreliable narrator: A narrator who, as we discover by a twist revelation at the end of the story, has manipulated or fabricated the preceding story, thus forcing the reader to question their prior assumptions about the text. This motif is often used within noir fiction and films, such as the films *The Usual Suspects* and *Shutter Island*.

Viewpoint: Point of view

Voice: The author's style, the quality that makes his or her writing unique and conveys the author's attitude, personality, and character; also: the characteristic speech and thought patterns of a first-person narrator or of a viewpoint character. Randy Ingermanson: "I'd define voice to be the 'attitude' you bring to your writing. This can be separated into the voice of each of your characters plus the voice you bring in as author."

Western fiction: A genre of fiction and films set in the American Old West frontier and typically set from the late eighteenth to the late nineteenth century.

THRILLERS – List of Subgenres with Examples

I've compiled a list of many of the subgenres of thrillers, and novels that fit (sometimes loosely) into the categories. Of course, many of the greatest thrillers defy subcategorizing, so don't worry about slotting in your thriller – just write a captivating, intriguing story! If you do decide to write a particular kind of thriller, however, be sure to do lots of reading in that subgenre to find out what's been done to death, and also the essential components of that subgenre. This list is primarily concerned with novels, not movies or TV shows.

Note that this list is by no means exhaustive. I've just named a handful of writers or titles under each category as good examples of the genre. If I've placed a book or author under the wrong category, please let me know, as I haven't read all these books! Also, if you feel there's a thriller that really must be included because of its superior quality and entertainment value, please pass that along and I'll try to add it. Thanks!

Also, you'll notice that some thrillers and thriller writers often overlap two or three subgenres.

First, a tip of the hat to these pioneers in the thriller genre:

EARLY THRILLERS (groundbreakers)

Homer's Odyssey, one of the oldest stories in the Western world, is considered an early prototype of the thriller.

The Count of Monte Cristo, by Alexandre Dumas (1844)

The Woman in White, by Wilkie Collins (1860)

The Strange Case of Dr. Jekyll and Mr. Hyde, by R. L. Stevenson (1886)

Dracula, by Bram Stoker (1897)

The War of the Worlds, by H. G. Wells (1898)

The Hound of the Baskervilles, by Sir Arthur Conan Doyle (1902)

The Thirty-Nine Steps, by John Buchan (1915)

ACTION-ADVENTURE THRILLERS

Emphasis on conflict and action rather than a complex plot or deep characterization. Usually feature a race against time, lots of violence and weapons, obvious villains, and practically nonstop action, with explosions, chase scenes, etc. Includes military or combat thrillers, which involve some branch of the military, usually special operations, and emphasize military tactics, combat, and weapons.

Pioneers of this subgenre:

Rogue Male, by Geoffrey Household (1939)

The Guns of Navarone, by Alistair MacLean (1957)

First Blood, by David Morrell (1972)

The Bourne Identity, by Robert Ludlum (1980)

Some popular action-adventure thrillers:

Shadow Divers, by Robert Kurson

Many of David Morrell's novels

Clive Cussler's series featuring character Dirk Pitt (also classified as techno-thrillers)

Many of Lee Child's Jack Reacher stories, such as: *Killing Floor, Die Trying, Tripwire, Running Blind, 61 Hours*, and *Worth Dying For*

Tom Clancy's books: *Clear and Present Danger, The Hunt for Red October*, and more.

The Lions of Lucerne, by Brad Thor

Dan Brown's books: *The Da Vinci Code, Angels & Demons*, etc.

Stieg Larsson's books: *The Girl with the Dragon Tattoo, The Girl Who Played with Fire*
Black Hawk Down, by Mark Bowden

BIOLOGICAL THRILLERS

A biological agent, such as a doomsday virus, is the major element in bio thrillers. Includes tales of biological warfare, biological disasters, or science-related thrillers. An outsider struggles against a powerful, sinister corporation or even the government to try to avert a cataclysmic disaster, which could be caused by a madman or by science going tragically awry.

A sampling of biological thrillers:

Jurassic Park, The Lost World, and *Prey*, by Michael Crichton
Neanderthal, by John Darnton
Mount Dragon, by Douglas & Lincoln Child
Bloodstream, by Tess Gerritsen
Whiteout, by Ken Follett
Ill Wind, by Kevin J. Anderson and Doug Beason
The Devil's Workshop, by Stephen J. Cannell
The First Horseman, by John Case
Vector, by Robin Cook
The Experiment, by John Darnton
Plum Island, by Nelson DeMille
White Plague, by Frank Herbert
The Blood Artists, by Chuck Hogan

CRIME THRILLERS

A less cerebral, more adrenaline-fused version of the "police procedural" of crime fiction. Often involve a police detective or, for more freedom and autonomy, an "off the leash" police officer/ detective or an ex-cop or ex-agent. All about committing crimes. Protagonists include present and retired or ex FBI agents, police homicide detectives, etc. Features a wide array of novels about revenge, blackmail, serial killers, forensic experts, psychologists, victims and criminals.

Some key authors, crime thrillers (in alphabetical order):

Ace Atkins, David Bowker, Allison Brennan, James Burke, Lee Child, Richard Condon, Robert Crais, Charles Fleming, Tess Gerritsen, Alex Kava, C.J. Lyons, James Patterson, Mario Puzo, J.D. Robb, Dan Simmons, Michael Walsh, and Stephen White

Popular crime thriller titles:

James Patterson's Alex Cross novels
J.D. Robb's Lieutenant Eve Dallas stories
C.J. Lyons' Lucy Guardino FBI thrillers
Out of Sight, by Elmore Leonard
The Apprentice, by Tess Gerritsen (2002)
Still Life with Crows, by Lincoln Child & Douglas Preston
Mafia Summer, by Vincent E. Duke
Dark End of the Street, by Ace Atkins
Godfather series, by Mario Puzo
Joe Kurtz series, by Dan Simmons
Hammerheads, by Dale Brown
Hostage, by Robert Crais
And All the Saints, by Michael Walsh
Midnight Runner, by Jack Higgins
Godfathers Revenge, by Mark Winegardner

ESPIONAGE OR SPY THRILLERS

Older spy thrillers made heavy use of the Cold War, the KGB, CIA, the British Secret Service and other international agencies. These days, political intrigue and heavy use of current events, such as the rise of terrorism, are the defining elements of these thrillers.

Pioneers in the subgenre:

Above Suspicion, by Helen Macinnes (1941)
Casino Royale, by Ian Fleming (1953) (Secret Agent James Bond)
From Russia, with Love, by Ian Fleming (1957) (James Bond)
The Ipcress File, by Len Deighton (1962) (Set in the Cold War)
The Spy Who Came In from the Cold, by John le Carré (1963)

Smiley's People, by John le Carré
Berlin Game, by Len Deighton (1983)
The Brotherhood of the Rose, by David Morrell (1984)

Some popular spy thriller titles:

The Unlikely Spy, by Daniel Silva
The Avenger, by Frederick Forsyth
Eye of the Needle, by Ken Follett
The Tears of Autumn, by Charles McCarry
Agent of Influence, by David Aaron
The Eleventh Commandment, by Jeffrey Archer
Jason Bourne series, by Robert Ludlum
Peter Ashton series, by Clive Egleton
The Day of the Jackal, by Frederick Forsyth
Sean Dillon series, by Jack Higgins
James Bond series, by Raymond Benson
James Bond series, by Ian Fleming
The Company of Strangers, by Robert Wilson
Wilderness of Mirrors, by Linda Davies

FINANCIAL / BUSINESS THRILLERS

Greed is the backbone of the action. Whether the story focuses on a sinister multinational corporation, a government conspiracy, embezzlement, or some sort of political corruption, money is at the heart of the problem. Often involves corporate power plays and outsmarting the competition. The villains are ruthless, with no holds barred.

Notable authors of financial thrillers:

Michael Crichton, Linda Davies, Jefferey Deaver, Paul Erdman, Joseph Finder, Stephen Frey, Philip Jolowicsz, Brad Meltzer, Richard K. Morgan, Katherine Neville, James Patterson, Christopher Reich, Michael M. Thomas, and Robert Wilson

Some popular business/finance thrillers:

The Chairman, Shadow Account, Silent Partner, The Day Trader,

Trust Fund, The Insider, and more, by Stephen Frey
Hanover Place, Hard Money, Someone Else's Money, and *Green Monday,* by Michael M. Thomas
The Devil's Banker and *Numbered Account,* by Christopher Reich
Rising Sun and *Disclosure,* by Michael Crichton
The Set-Up and *The Last Days of America,* by Paul Erdman
Paranoia and *Company Man,* by Joseph Finder
A Calculated Risk, by Katherine Neville
A Small Death in Lisbon, by Robert Wilson
Nest of Vipers, by Linda Davies
Mistress of Justice, by Jeffrey Deaver
Walls of Silence, by Philip Jolowicsz
The Shadow Box, by John R. Maxim
The Millionaires, by Brad Meltzer
Market Forces, by Richard K. Morgan
Black Market, by James Patterson

HISTORICAL THRILLERS

Often concerned with activity involved around great wars or other tense, pivotal periods in the history of the world. Sometimes take liberties with actual historical events.

Some well-known authors of historical thrillers:

John C. Berry, Steve Berry, Caleb Carr, Michael Crichton, Jeffery Deaver, Robert Harris, Greg Iles, D.L. Johnstone, Raymond Khoury, Carolyn McCray, Glenn Meade, David Morrell, Terrence O'Brien, James Rollins, and M.J. Rose

A sampling of historical thriller authors and titles:

James Rollins: *The Doomsday Key, Altar of Eden, The Judas Strain,* and many more
Steve Berry: *The Romanov Prophecy, The Columbus Affair, The Templar Legacy, The Alexandria Link, The Venetian Betrayal, The Charlemagne Pursuit, The Paris Vendetta,* etc.
Raymond Khoury: *The Last Templar, The Sanctuary,* etc.
Matthew Reilly: *Seven Deadly Wonders, The Six Sacred Stones,*

The Five Greatest Warriors, and more
Murder as a Fine Art, and *Last Reveille*, by David Morrell
Pirate Latitudes, by Michael Crichton
The Second Messiah, by Glenn Meade
Fatherland, by Robert Harris
The Angel of Darkness, by Caleb Carr
A Gathering of Spies, by John Altman (WW II spies)
The Secret Supper: A Novel, by Javier Sierra
Garden of Beasts, by Jeffery Deaver
The Alexander Cipher, by Will Adams
Instruments of Darkness, by Imogen Robertson
Black Cross, by Greg Iles
The Hypnotist, by M. J. Rose
Sovereign, by C. J. Sansom

HORROR THRILLERS

A hybrid between horror and thriller novels. Preys on our deepest fears. Emphasis on scaring the readers/viewers. Nasty, powerful, frightening villains.

A sampling of authors of horror thrillers:

Stephen King, Thomas Harris, Dean Koontz, Anne Rice, Joe Hill, Max Brooks, William Peter Blatty

Some well-known horror thriller novels:

Stephen King's novels: *The Shining, Cujo, The Stand, Christine, Misery, Pet Sematary*, and many others
The Silence of the Lambs, by Thomas Harris
Jaws, by Peter Benchley
Evergreen, by David Jester
Creepers, by David Morrell

INTERNATIONAL THRILLERS

These thrillers take you all over the world. Great for the armchair traveler!

Steve Berry's novels
Many of James Patterson's novels
The Orphan Trilogy and other Orphan novels, by James Morcan and Lance Morcan
The Bank of Fear, by David Ignatius
Buddha Kiss, by Peter Tasker
Black Money, by Michael M. Thomas
Wilderness of Mirrors, by Linda Davies
Rising Sun, by Michael Crichton
No Remorse, by Ian Walkley
The Blade, by Lynn Sholes & Joe Moore

LEGAL THRILLERS

One of the most popular types of thrillers, the action centers on courtroom drama, as a lawyer must use his/her intellect to overcome adversity or save a client, and is often threatened or placed in danger. The protagonist can also be a judge or law student, but is usually a defense lawyer.

Pioneer: Presumed Innocent, by Scott Turow (1987)

Some authors of popular legal thrillers, in alphabetical order:

David Baldacci, William Bernhardt, Robert Dugoni, Dominick Dunne, David Ellis, Linda Fairstein, James Grippando, John Grisham, William Lashner, John Lescroart, Phillip Margolin, Steve Martini, Brad Meltzer, Richard North Patterson, Lisa Scottoline, Robert Tanenbraun, Scott Turow, Kate Wilhelm, and Stuart Woods

A sampling of popular legal thrillers:

John Grisham's novels: *The Firm, The Last Juror, A Time to Kill, The Confession*, and many more
Michael Connelly's Lincoln Lawyer novels
False Witness, by Lelia Kelly
Wild Justice, by Phillip Margolin
Past Due, by William Lashner

In the Shadow of the Law, by Kermit Roosevelt
Murder One, The Jury Master, and other novels by Robert Dugoni
Lisa Scottoline's novels, like *Daddy's Girl, Dirty Blonde, Courting Trouble*

MEDICAL THRILLERS

Usually set in a hospital or research center, with bad things happening to patients. Authors and main characters are often medical professionals.

Some key authors of medical thrillers, in alphabetical order:

Gary Braver, John Case, April Christofferson, Peter Clement, Robin Cook, Patricia Cornwell, Michael Crichton, John Darnton, Eileen Dreyer, Tess Gerritsen, Leonard S. Goldberg, DP Lyle, CJ Lyons, Michael Palmer, Kathy Reichs, Steven Spruill, Stephen White, F. Paul Wilson

Popular medical thriller titles:

Coma, by Robin Cook
The Surgeon, by Tess Gerritsen
Harvest, by Tess Gerritsen
Do No Harm, by Greg Andrew Hurwitz
Fear Nothing, by Dean Koontz
The Cobra Event, by Richard Preston
When the Wind Blows, by James Patterson
The Tangled Web, by Ken McClure
Chromosome 6, by Robin Cook

NOIR OR HARD-BOILED CRIME THRILLERS

These thrillers have their roots in film noir crime dramas of the late thirties to late fifties. Protagonist is usually a police detective or private investigator who has witnessed too much crime, especially organized crime, combined with a corrupt legal system, and has become hardened and cynical. Closely related to hard-boiled mysteries.

Pioneers in noir thrillers:

Raymond Chandler
Dashiell Hammett
The Postman Always Rings Twice, by James M. Cain (1934)
The Killer Inside Me, by Jim Thompson (1952)

Some current authors of noir thrillers:

Megan E. Abbott, Kent Anderson, Mitchell Bartoy, David Bowker, James Lee Burke, Ken Bruen, Michael Chabon, James Crumley, Pete Dexter, John Dobbyn, Loren D. Estleman, Jim Fusilli, Andrew Klavan, Peter Macklin, Cormac McCarthy, and Michael Tolkin

A sampling of neo-noir thrillers:

The Guards, The Priest, The Dramatist, Bust, and more by Ken Bruen
Die a Little, and *The Song Is You*, by Megan E. Abbott
Night Dogs, by Kent Anderson
The Devil's Own Rag Doll, by Mitchell Bartoy
No Country for Old Men, by Cormac McCarthy
The Player, by Michael Tolkin

PARANORMAL OR SUPERNATURAL THRILLERS

Either the protagonist or the antagonist may possess special powers or supernatural abilities.

Carrie, It, and other thrillers by Stephen King
Many of Dean Koontz's novels, like his Odd series
Many of James Patterson's novels
Jaws, by Peter Benchley
Bangkok Haunts, by John Burdett
The Lovely Bones, by Alice Sebold

Some other authors of paranormal thrillers:

John Connolly, Ted Dekker, Heather Graham, Kay Hooper, Michael Koryta, Patrick Lee, Douglas Preston & Lincoln Child, Anne Rice, and more

POLITICAL THRILLERS

Some key authors of political thrillers (in alphabetical order):

David Baldacci, Tom Clancy, Ben Coes, Stephen Coonts, Vince Flynn, Stephen Frey, Tim Green, Jack Higgins, Robert Ludlum, Phillip Margolin, Brad Meltzer, Oliver North, Richard North Patterson, Joel C. Rosenberg, Brad Thor, Stuart Woods, and Sidney Sheldon

Popular political thriller titles

Vince Flynn – *Transfer of Power, Executive Power*, and many more.
Tom Clancy – *Patriot Games, The Hunt for Red October, Clear and Present Danger*, etc.
David Baldacci – *The Camel Club, Stone Cold, Hell's Corner, True Blue*
The Pardon and *The Abduction*, by James Grippando
The Legacy and *The Fourth Order*, by Stephen Frey
Rising Sun, by Michael Crichton
The Good German, by Joseph Kanon
The Bourne Identity, by Robert Ludlum
The President's Assassin, by Brian Haig
Capital Crimes, by Stuart Woods
Shot, by Phillip Kerr
The Hunters, by W.E.B. Griffin
Exile, by Richard North Patterson
Capitol Threat, by William Bernhardt
The First Commandment, by Brad Thor
Parallax View, by Allan Leverone

PSYCHOLOGICAL THRILLERS

If you prefer mind games over chase scenes, go for psychological suspense, with its heavy focus on the unstable emotional states of characters.

Pioneers and groundbreakers:

La Bête Humaine, by Emile Zola (1890)
Laura, by Vera Caspary (1943)
The Collector, by John Fowles (1963)
The Shining, by Stephen King (1977)
When the Bough Breaks, by Jonathan Kellerman (1981)
The Silence of the Lambs, by Thomas Harris (1988)
Rules of Prey, by John Sandford (1989)
American Psycho, by Bret Easton Ellis (1991)
Patricia Highsmith's novels

Some authors of psychological thrillers:

Desmond Cory, Emma Donoghue, Gillian Flynn, Nicci French, Tana French, Rod Glenn, Jonathan Kellerman, Mary Higgins Clark, Thomas Harris, Henry James, Andrew E. Kaufman, Stephen King, Stieg Larsson, Dennis Lehane, Jeff Menapace, Chuck Palahniuk, Paul Parducci, Aleatha Romig, R.D. Ronald, Orson Scott Card, S.J. Watson, Melanie Wells, and Louise Welsh

Popular psychological thrillers:

Gone Girl, by Gillian Flynn
Shutter Island, by Dennis Lehane
Red Dragon and *Hannibal*, by Thomas Harris
The Girl with the Dragon Tattoo, by Stieg Larsson
The Lion, the Lamb, the Hunted, by Andrew E. Kaufman
Before I Go to Sleep, by S.J. Watson
Consequences and *Truth*, by Aleatha Romig
In the Woods, by Tana French
Room, by Emma Donoghue
Fight Club, by Chuck Palahniuk

ROMANTIC THRILLERS (romantic suspense)

More character-driven, involve relationships. Usually two protagonists, one male, one female, who become involved with each other. Usually have a happily-ever-after ending.

Pioneers:

Rebecca, by Daphne du Maurier (1938)
The Rendezvous, by Evelyn Anthony (1967)

Some of the many popular authors of romantic suspense, in alphabetical order:

Cherry Adair, Kristen Ashley, Cate Beauman, Allison Brennan, Suzanne Brockman, Sandra Brown, Linda Castillo, Pamela Clare, Claire Contreras, Jordan Dane, Silvia Day, Kendra Elliot, Janet Evanovich, Marie Force, Barbara Freethy, Cindy Gerard, Alexa Grace, Heather Graham, Linda Howard, Julie James, Lisa Renee Jones, Melinda Leigh, Carla Neggers, Brenda Novak, J.D. Robb, Nora Roberts, T.E. Sivec, Nicholas Sparks, Roxanne St. Claire, Erica Stevens, Colleen Thompson

A sampling of popular romantic thrillers:

Sandra Brown's novels of the past 20 years or so: *Smash Cut, Smoke Screen, Ricochet, The Alibi,* etc.

Nora Roberts' romantic suspense novels, such as these, all of which have won awards: *Brazen Virtue: Night Shift, Divine Evil, Nightshade, Hidden Riches, Carolina Moon, Three Fates,* and *Remember When – Part 1*; and, as J.D. Robb, *Survivor in Death* and *New York to Dallas*

Janet Evanovich's Stephanie Plum novels

Pamela Clare's I-Team series

SPECULATIVE AND FUTURISTIC THRILLERS

A thriller set in the future, often action or combat stories. Usually the antagonist or villain embodies futuristic qualities, while the hero is someone we can very easily relate to.

The Andromeda Strain, by Michael Crichton (1969)

Jurassic Park, by Michael Crichton
Mammoth, by John Varley (2005)
The Gauntlet Assassin, by L.J. Sellers

STRONG FEMALE PROTAGONISTS IN THRILLERS

Who are some spunky, kick-ass female leads in thrillers? Here's a sampling of popular ones:

Allison Brennan's Lucy Kincaid
J.D. Robb's Detective Eve Dallas
The Maggie O'Dell series by Alex Kava
Irene Kelly, the journalist from Jan Burke's series
Tess Gerritsen's Rizzoli & Isles series
Zoe Sharp's Charlie Fox.
Claire Randall in the Outlander series by Diana Gabaldon
Anna Pigeon from Nevada Barr's novels
Eve Duncan series by Iris Johansen
Lisa Gardner's Detective D.D. Warren
Lara Evans in *The Gauntlet Assassin*, by L.J. Sellers
Katniss in *The Hunger Games*, by Suzanne Collins
Tracie Tanner in Allan Leverone's *Parallax View*
The heroines of thrillers by Sandra Brown, Suzanne Collins, Lisa Gardner, Tess Gerritsen, Heather Graham, Lisa Jackson, Alex Kava, Laura Lippman, Lisa Scottoline, Karin Slaughter, Veronica Roth, and many more

Supernatural Thrillers – see Paranormal Thrillers

TECHNO-THRILLERS

Huge on technical details, especially military technology. Explore the inner workings of technology and the mechanics of various disciplines (espionage, martial arts, military, politics). Emphasis on real-world or plausible near-future technology.

Two authors defined the techno-thriller genre with these novels:

Michael Crichton, *The Andromeda Strain* (1969)

Tom Clancy, *The Hunt for Red October* (1984)

Other early examples:

Moonraker, by Ian Fleming (1955)
Fail-Safe, by Eugene Burdick and Harvey Wheeler (1962)
The Penetrators, by Hank Searls (writing as Anthony Grey) (1965)
Tree Frog, by Martin Woodhouse (1966)
North Cape, by Joe Poyer (1969)
Firefox, by Craig Thomas (1977)
Shuttle Down, by G. Harry Stine (writing as Lee Correy) (1981)

Significant contemporary techno-thriller authors:

Larry Bond, Dale Brown, Dan Brown, Joe Buff, Caleb Carr, Richard Condon, Douglas Preston and Lincoln Child, Tom Clancy, Stephen Coonts, Harold Coyle, Michael Crichton, Clive Cussler, Len Deighton, Bill DeSmedt, Greg Dinallo, Cory Doctorow, Jeff Edwards, John Gardner, Peter F. Hamilton, Eric L. Harry, Ben Kay, Brian Schan, Philip Kerr, Robert Ludlum, Jonathan Maberry, Alistair MacLean, Eric Nylund, Stel Pavlou, Ralph Peters, James Clancy Phelan, Matthew Reilly, Patrick Robinson, James Rollins, Neal Stephenson, Daniel Suarez, Walter Wager

Popular techno-thriller titles:

The Hammer of Eden, by Ken Follett
Killing Time, by Caleb Carr
The Blue Nowhere, by Jeffery Deaver
Call to Duty, by Richard Harman
Cold Fall, by John Gardner
Neuromancer, by William Gibson
Sword Point, by Harold Coyle
Darwin's Children, by Greg Bear
Digital Fortress, by Dan Brown
The Bear and the Dragon, by Tom Clancy
Cyclops One, by Jim DeFelice
Utopia, by Lincoln Child

TRUE-CRIME THRILLERS

In Cold Blood, by Truman Capote (1966)
Alive: The Story of the Andes Survivors, by Piers Paul Read (1974)
Green River, Running Red, by Ann Rule (2004)

YOUNG ADULT (YA) THRILLERS

The Hunger Games, by Suzanne Collins
Playing Tyler, by T.L. Costa
Monkey Wars, by Richard Kurti
Acceleration, by Graham McNamee
Frost, by Marianna Baer
What We Saw at Night, by Jacquelyn Mitchard
The Diviners, by Libba Bray
Cryer's Cross, by Lisa McMann
Ten, by Gretchen McNeil

Resources:
Amazon lists
Goodreads lists
Library Thing
Overbooked.com: http://www.overbooked.org/booklists/genres/
Thrillers – A Guide for Readers' Advisors, by Radenka Vidovic and David Hansen, https://www.library.ns.ca/files/thrillers_1.pdf
Thrillers – 100 Must-Reads
The Best Thrillers of All Time, *Reader's Digest*, http://www.rd.com/advice/the-best-thriller-books-of-all-time/
What is a Thriller? 2004, Metropolitan Library System: http://www.mls.lib.il.us/consulting/ra/ra_thrillers.asp
The Compulsive Reader: www.thecompulsivereader.com
Wikipedia

RESOURCES FOR CRIME FICTION WRITERS

CRAFT-OF-WRITING GUIDES

Here are some excellent writing guides, listed alphabetically by author:

Bell, James Scott, *Revision & Self-Editing – Techniques for transforming your first draft into a finished novel*

Bell, James Scott, *Conflict & Suspense*

Bell, James Scott, *Plot & Structure*

Bickham, Jack M., *The 38 Most Common Fiction Writing Mistakes (And How to Avoid Them)*

Bickham, Jack M., *Writing and Selling Your Novel*

Block, Lawrence, *Writing the Novel*

Bradbury, Ray, *Zen in the Art of Writing: Releasing the Creative Genius Within You*

Browne, Renni and Dave King, *Self-Editing for Fiction Writers – How to Edit Yourself into Print*

Card, Orson Scott, *Characters & Viewpoint – Elements of Fiction Writing*

Egri, Lajos, *The Art of Creative Writing*

Ephron, Hallie, *The Everything Guide to Writing Your First Novel*

Frey, James N., *How to Write a Damn Good Mystery*

Frey, James N., *How to Write a Damn Good Novel, I & II*

Frey, James N., *How to Write a Damn Good Thriller*

Gardner, John, *On Becoming a Novelist*

Goldberg, Natalie, *Writing Down the Bones*
Ingermanson, Randy & Peter Economy, *Writing Fiction for Dummies*
King, Stephen, *On Writing – A Memoir of the Craft*
Koontz, Dean, *How to Write Best-Selling Fiction*
Lamott, Anne, *Bird by Bird, Some Instructions on Writing and Life*
Lukeman, Noah, *The First Five Pages – A Writer's Guide to Staying out of the Rejection Pile*
Lyon, Elizabeth, *Manuscript Makeover – Revision Techniques No Fiction Writer Can Afford to Ignore*
Lyon, Elizabeth, *A Writer's Guide to Fiction*
Maass, Donald, *Writing the Breakout Novel*
Maass, Donald, *The Fire in Fiction*
McKee, Robert, *Story: Substance, Structure, Style, and the Principles of Screenwriting*
Morrell, David, *The Successful Novelist*
Morrell, Jessica Page, *Thanks, But This Isn't For Us, A (Sort of) Compassionate Guide to Why Your Writing is Being Rejected*
Morrell, Jessica Page, *Between the Lines – the subtle elements of fiction writing*
Stein, Sol, *Stein on Writing*
Swain, Dwight V., *Techniques of the Selling Writer*
Whitney, Phyllis, *Guide to Fiction Writing*
Wiesner, Karen S., *From First Draft to Finished Novel*

ORGANIZATIONS

International Thriller Writers – an honorary society of authors who write books broadly classified as "thrillers." This would include murder mystery, detective, suspense, horror, supernatural, action, espionage, true crime, war, and action-adventure. ITW brings together almost 1000 writers, readers, publishers, editors and agents at its annual conference, ThrillerFest, as well as at CraftFest, a writing workshop program, and AgentFest, where aspiring authors can meet and pitch top literary agents.

Mystery Writers of America – MWA, founded in 1945, is the premier organization for mystery and crime writers, professionals allied to the crime writing field, aspiring crime writers, and folks who just love to read crime fiction. Each spring, they present the prestigious Edgar® Awards. MWA also helps to rebuild libraries and offers numerous symposiums and events for both authors and fans.

Sisters in Crime – SinC has 3600 members in 48 chapters worldwide, offering networking, advice and support to mystery authors. Members are authors, readers, publishers, agents, booksellers and librarians who love the mystery genre and want to support women who write mysteries. Membership is also open to men.

Crime Writers of Canada – CWC is a national association for Canadian mystery and crime writers, associated professionals, and others with a serious interest in Canadian crime writing. Promotes Canadian crime writing. Newsletter, information on authors, awards, and links. The CWC has sponsored Canada's Arthur Ellis Awards for Crime and Mystery Writing since 1984.

Crime Writers of Great Britain – A professional body which sets out to represent writers of crime fiction and non-fiction. The CWA has played a major role both in discovering and supporting the careers of many of Britain's finest writers, including PD James, Ian Rankin, Frederick Forsyth, Ruth Rendell, Val McDermid and Alexander McCall Smith. Presents the annual prestigious CWA Dagger Awards to recognize quality in today's crime and thriller fiction writing.

CONFERENCES, CONVENTIONS, and WORKSHOPS FOR CRIME WRITERS

Thrillerfest and Craftfest – International Thriller Writers annual conference, New York, NY, July. A four-day celebration of suspense-thriller novels, the authors who write them, and the fans who read them. Includes Craftfest, the first day and a half, crammed with excellent craft workshops to choose from presented by bestselling authors, and Agentfest, a half-day of pitching to as many agents as you can cram in. Thrillerfest, the last two days, features excellent panel discussions on various topics.

Bouchercon Crime Fiction Convention – Annual world mystery convention, open to anyone; a place for fans, authors and professionals to gather and celebrate their love of the mystery genre. Usually held in October. Includes book-signings, panels, discussions, and interviews with authors and people from the mystery community covering all parts of the genre. Anthony Awards, named after Anthony Boucher, presented at the convention.

Love is Murder Conference – The Love is Murder Mystery Authors, Readers and Fans Con is always Super Bowl weekend, at the Intercontinental O'Hare Hotel, just outside of Chicago. Draws more than 300 writers and readers from the U.S., Canada, and overseas. Features panel discussions, author signings, demonstrations, Lovey awards banquet, entertainment, and opportunities to meet mystery authors and network with other readers and fans.

Writers' Police Academy, Jamestown, NC. The Writers' Police Academy offers the most hands-on, interactive and educational experience writers can find to enhance their understanding of all aspects of law enforcement and forensics. This is a one of a kind event, featuring real police, fire, and EMS training at an actual police academy. Top instructors and experts!

The New England Crime Bake Conference, Dedham, Mass, just outside Boston, in November. An annual conference celebrating the work of New England crime fiction and nonfiction authors. Features panels, seminars, and interviews with authors, literary agents, and experts in forensics and other fields related to crime writing, as well as classes on writing craft, manuscript critiques, and book signing events.

Cape Fear Crime Festival – New Hanover Library, Wilmington, NC, February. The festival is an intimate gathering for writers to learn about the craft of writing and promotion with other writing professionals.

Left Coast Crime Mystery Convention – An annual mystery convention sponsored by mystery fans, for mystery fans. It is held during the first quarter of the calendar year in Western North

America, as defined by the Mountain Time Zone and all time zones westward to Hawaii.

Malice Domestic – An annual traditional mystery fan convention held in Bethesda, MD, in May. Malice Domestic is an annual "fun fan" convention in metropolitan Washington, D.C., saluting the traditional mystery—books best typified by the works of Agatha Christie. The genre is loosely defined as mysteries which contain no explicit sex or excessive gore or violence.

CrimeFest, Bristol, UK – First organised in June 2008, CrimeFest has become one of the most popular dates in the crime fiction calendar. The annual convention draws top crime novelists, readers, editors, publishers and reviewers from around the world and gives delegates the opportunity to celebrate the genre in an informal atmosphere. Includes author panels, crime writing workshops, a pitch-an-agent strand, etc.

Public Safety Writers Conference, Las Vegas, Nevada. Open to those writing fiction or nonfiction about or for any public safety field. Conference speakers include a coroner, fire fighters, police officers, and others in the writing field.

A FEW WORDS FROM THE AUTHOR

I'd love to hear from you. If my tips here have inspired you to make your story more powerful by introducing more tension, conflict, suspense and intrigue, it would be great if you could write a short review of this book on the Amazon page. If you have any suggestions for this book or future ones, please contact me by email at Info@JodieRenner.com. Thanks!

Please look for my longer, more detailed book on style, pacing, and voice, called *Fire up Your Fiction*, which is filled with before-and-after examples from my editing. I will soon be publishing more books on other aspects of writing compelling fiction, such *Those Critical First Five Pages*, *Powerful Point of View*, and *Bring Your Story to Life*, so I hope you'll come back in a few months and look for them. Thanks!

Keep on writing! I look forward to reading your compelling suspense fiction!

– Jodie Renner,
June 2013

ABOUT THE AUTHOR

Jodie Renner is a freelance fiction editor who specializes in thrillers, romantic suspense, mysteries, and other crime fiction, as well as mainstream, young adult, and historical fiction.

Jodie taught English (and French) for many years, and has a master's degree in literature, as well as a lifelong passion for reading well-written, compelling fiction.

Some of Jodie's favorite authors include Robert Crais, Sandra Brown, Lee Child, Lisa Gardner, Dean Koontz, Nora Roberts, Michael Connelly, Lisa Scottoline, John Grisham, Allison Brennan, Harlan Coben, Karin Slaughter, and Janet Evanovich.

Jodie's craft-of-fiction articles appear regularly or from time to time on the following blogs: Crime Fiction Collective, The Writer's Forensics Blog, Jodie Renner Editing, The Kill Zone, Blood-Red Pencil, The Thrill Begins, and Mystery Writing is Murder, as well as others.

When she's not reading novels or editing books, Jodie loves to pursue her two other main passions, traveling and photography. In fact, Jodie loves traveling so much she's thinking of changing her tagline from "Let's work together to enhance and empower your writing," to "Have laptop, will travel."

Permission has been granted for passages quoted, from:

* Andrew Gross, for a passage from *Don't Look Twice*
* Lynn Sholes and Joe Moore, for a passage from *The Blade*
* David Morrell, for a passage from *The Brotherhood of the Rose*
* Andrew E. Kaufman, for a passage from *The Lion, The Lamb, The Hunted*
* Dennis Lehane's agent, for a passage from *Shutter Island*
* James N. Frey, for quotes and ideas from *How to Write a Damn Good Thriller*

BONUS PAGES

A sample chapter, "Voice," from Jodie's style book:

Fire up Your Fiction
An Editor's Guide to Writing Compelling Stories

Available in paperback, for Kindle, and in other e-book formats

"This book is packed with good advice on how to spot and fix weaknesses in your fiction writing. It summarizes the combined wisdom of the last century or so of fiction teachers into one handy volume."
– Randy Ingermanson, bestselling author of *Writing Fiction for Dummies*

"A handy checklist and self-editing guide that will get any fiction writer to a stronger, well-told tale."
– James Scott Bell, bestselling author of *Revision & Self-Editing*, *Plot & Structure*, and *The Art of War for Writers*

Sample chapter from Fire up Your Fiction:

Chapter 11 – VOICE: THAT ELUSIVE BUT CRITICAL INGREDIENT OF COMPELLING FICTION

Voice – what is it exactly?

Literary agents and acquiring editors always say they're looking for fiction with a compelling, unique, fresh, natural voice. Then when asked to define it, they hum and haw a bit, searching for the right words to try to capture what they mean by a voice that appeals to readers and makes them want to keep reading.

From what I've gathered from my varied reading and workshops, the ideal "voice" is that natural, open, appealing, charismatic tone and style that draws us in and makes us feel like we know the characters well – and want to get to know them better!

HOW CAN WE DEVELOP AN APPEALING VOICE?

These tips, a mix of advice from others and my own ideas, will be helpful to both fiction and nonfiction writers who are still in the process of finding their voice or fine-tuning it to make it more relaxed, powerful and appeal*ing*.

Don't lecture your readers.
As Bruce DeSilva said in his workshop on this topic at Craftfest 2012, many aspiring authors need to first free themselves from the constraints of their more formal, correct writing background, especially if it includes graduate degrees and a lot of legal, academic or business writing. So shake yourself loose of all those constraints and find your more casual, accessible, appealing inner voice. How do you do that?

Write in a clear, direct way.
Forget all those long, convoluted sentences and pretentious words and learn to write in a clear, direct, accessible, casual style that evokes the senses and appeals to the emotions. Streamline your writing!

Write to one person.
To help develop an intimacy with your readership and a conversational tone, create or choose one single person you're writing to, who is warm, friendly, open to your ideas, interested, and intelligent.

DeSilva suggests choosing a close friend or family member to write to, but personally, I advise against writing to someone in your inner circle, as you might end up skipping over a lot of details and points that need to be there for other readers who don't share your background, cultural environment, and basic frames of reference.

So I suggest creating an ideal reader. Write a brief description of their age, gender, background, home and work situation, personality, and interests (which of course include reading your kind of writing!). Get to know them a bit by giving them some positive attributes that will help you feel comfortable and open with them. Then target your writing to this person. Relax and let the real you come through.

Read and imitate writers whose voice you really enjoy.

Don't copy their words verbatim, of course, but immerse yourself in their story world, told in their unique voice. Read their books aloud to really internalize the rhythm of their language, the phrasing and expressions and word choices that appeal to you so much. Then of course adapt the cadence and rhythm and attitudes and vocabulary to your own situation.

Write a chapter in first person, then change it to third person.

One author whose voice I love is Janet Evanovich, whose spunky, quirky heroine, Stephanie Plum, narrates her story in first-person point of view. But it's hard to write first-person well, and it can be limiting, as you're confined to scenes where this character is present. Also, first-person isn't always the best choice for, say, a thriller, as you want other viewpoints in there, too, notably that of the antagonist.

But try writing several pages or a chapter or two in first-person ("I"), to develop your main character's unique voice, then just go back and rewrite them in third person (he/she), with as few other changes as possible.

Read your story out loud to test its authenticity and easy flow.

As DeSilva says, writing should have the rhythm and comfortable familiarity of spoken language. If it doesn't flow easily, go in and streamline the language to take out the convoluted sentences, clunky phrasing, and fancy-shmancy words. Or hire a trusted writer friend or reputable freelance editor to go through it for you to take out anything that sounds too formal, wordy, or erudite.

Write in deep point of view or close third.
This means the story is unfolding mainly through the thoughts and reactions and emotions and attitudes of your protagonist. Even descriptions of your setting should be filtered through your protagonist's (or other viewpoint character's) preferences, views, and mood. This ensures that your whole novel has a great, unique voice, not just the dialogue.

Give each character his or her own voice.
When you're writing dialogue, each character should sound different, with their own unique speech patterns, word choices, and slang or pet expressions, based on their milieu, upbringing, education, and personality. Listen in on all kinds of conversations, both in real life and on TV and in movies.

Develop an ear for how different people speak. To improve the idiosyncratic speech of a character in your novel, try journaling in their voice, in first person. Just write freely, using lots of attitude! Eventually, you'll get into their rhythm and find the words that seem to suit them best.

So break free from the constraints of your background, education, and any more formal work-related writing, and write the story only you can write, with your unique experiences and personality, in your own direct, open, interesting voice. Don't hold back – reveal yourself.

Made in the USA
Charleston, SC
27 July 2014